Finding Meaning at the Movies

Sara Anson Vaux

Abingdon Press
Nashville

FINDING MEANING AT THE MOVIES

This book is printed on acid-free paper.

Library of Congress Cataloging-in-Publicaton Data

Vaux, Sara Anson.
    Finding meaning at the movies / Sara Anson Vaux.
        p.   cm.
    Includes bibliographical references.
    ISBN 0-687-06721-9 (alk. paper)
        1. Motion pictures—Moral and ethical aspects.   2. Motion pictures—
Religious aspects—Christianity.   I. Title.
PN1995.5.V28   1998
791.43'653—dc21   98-33176
                                                                          CIP

To Joan Fromm Greenstone and
Carole Frey Hettinger —
you lived Kingdom lives

99 00 01 02 03 04 05 06 07 08—10 9 8 7 6 5 4 3 2 1

MANUFACTURED IN THE UNITED STATES OF AMERICA

Contents

APPENDIX TWO

Storytelling

The Magic and Morality of the Movies

Film is a powerfully evocative art: Movies not only mirror our desires and dreams, they also shape them as we struggle to understand ourselves and our world. The following reflections express my feelings about the power of story, as mediated through movies.

A PERSONAL NOTE

Many years ago, a father of small children, brilliant creator of an acclaimed new novel, killed himself. I don't remember the event. I only remember the telling of the story. One day my kind and normally preoccupied mother drove me down a dusty country road canopied with the sycamores and hickories that flourished in this southern county's thick, black muck. She pulled our old Studebaker off to the side of the road, cleared her throat, and said: "Bob was a good man. The church people are partly to blame because they said awful things about the stories and ideas in his book. He heard them, and it wounded him. How can they live with that?"

It was my first lesson in evil. I was a barely reasoning eight-year-old, undiscriminating and unsuspecting. For me, people and things had only one face. Every Sunday the rest of that summer I sat in church beside my mother, wondering which of those trim, dour ladies or men had spoken the words that hurt a man who thought, wrote, and looked very much like my own daddy. When, a few years later, I studied Matthew 23:27-28 in Sunday school, I mentally connected the words *whited sepulchre* and *scribes and Pharisees* to the white limestone front of that church, with its (alleged) evil-speakers inside.

It was also my first lesson in the power and the threat of art: the strength of words not simply to say, but to suggest — words and images that can ignite memory's fires or twist a novel's rich metaphors to slander. Story and myth, as theologian Dorothee Soelle has reminded us, recall lost times or forgotten experience; they can evoke the power of divinity. Story and myth can also call forth our fears — our personal demons — and exorcise them one by one. The demons brought to light in that majestic novel written by a soon-to-be shattered novelist were ones never acknowledged in this sleepy half-southern town where we summered: the demons of racism, (so-called) miscegenation, and ethnic extermination.

My mother and father fought racism all their lives and thought *miscegenation* applied only to Protestants dating Catholics. For all other persons under the warm summer sun, they could live and love as they wished. But for the third demon, ethnic extermination, my father knew as well as anyone the details of the "removal" of indigenous tribes — Miami and Potawatomi Indians — from our state. He knew descendants of the survivors of that action. He knew tribal chiefs. As a boy growing up on a farm, he had seen firsthand the fragments of those lost lives. Shards of supper dishes, arrowheads, tools had popped out of the earth with almost every turn of his plow. Happily exiled from the farm by his supportive brother and sister, my father set about to discover what had happened to the men—and to their wives and children—who had once hunted and farmed his part of the Midwest.

The young novelist my mother had told me about had not set out to write a sermon or to expose the sins that generations in his home state had overlaid with greedy acquisitions and propriety; he had set out to write a good book, a book that the history he had uncovered compelled him to create. The suffering of a different time became his own, and he conveyed its particular fascination and horror through language.

My mother's storytelling registers in my memory as being this same kind of loving act, the mark of her ability to separate good actions from harmful ones. Like the wise men and women of ancient times, a mother had said to her child: "A person like you and me was alive and loved and hopeful. It makes me cry when I think that he was sad. The world should not be like this." I was changed by her words.

Literature and film can be like those tellings, both purposeful and poetic. Recent research into the development of infants' brains proves what grandmothers and grandfathers have always known: It is not simply the *sounds* of words (from radio or television or parents chattering to adult friends) but their *intent* (a parent speaking to a child, an "I" to a "thou") that activates the sensory pathways and stimulates feeling, emotion, and response.[1] Not just any words will do. Words and images organized by and for persons with names, histories, and futures—these are the stories we remember and honor.[2]

The movies we will examine in this book are among those thousands created some time in the last one hundred years to "delight and instruct"—Sir Philip Sidney's sixteenth-century catchphrase for the role of poetry. One thread unifies the films presented here: They are all, in some way, versions of that story my mother told me a half-century ago. In other words, they are deliberate attempts to communicate a concept of a moral universe—a sense of order and meaning that affects the ways we live on and with our earth; a search to determine right or wrong behavior; and a grasp of how we should behave toward one another. Underlying my mother's story and these films is a feeling of wholeness, lying somewhere back in memory, that is sometimes expressed as innocence, a good place to be, or love without price—dearly bought and openly shared. This wholeness assumes a universe in which human values are affirmed even in the midst of suffering and loss. The stories lie in the space between the "is" and the "ought"—the space between who we are as believers and actors in this world, and who and where we want to be.

In many cases the character whose story is being told in a movie, such as Bud in *Wall Street,* is not aware of loss or alienation. After all, such ideas are defined by absence: loss of goodness, purity, or direction; or alienation from a true self, from the family, or from nature. The absence may not be felt until the presence of another way of life is known. This absence is not so much a fall from some original purity or goodness (a golden age that we are trying to recover) as it is a discovery of a new version of life, a new definition of wholeness that takes its energy from the love of God and the doing of God's work in the world with "God's hands."[3]

Such wholeness is never forgotten, and yet it remains to be discovered. This wholeness, this place we're looking for, is the home where our true self resides, a self that gains strength from God and gives birth to moral acts of justice, mercy, and love. It is a present, indwelling kingdom of God—the compelling idea, thoroughly grounded in the Hebrew Scriptures, that finds radiant expression in Jesus' miracles, healing, and teachings. As the priest says to the newly married couple in *The Tree of the Wooden Clogs,* "Paradise starts with the love we show each other here on earth." How that paradise—that kingdom—makes itself known will be dramatized by the movies presented and discussed herein.

How to Use This Book

Use the table of contents in the front of the book to locate chapters and parts of the book by page number. Each chapter begins by listing the major theme and the main films discussed. This is followed by an introduction to the chapter, which establishes the significance of the theme, and by reflections, in which we begin to explore that theme and its relation to the films. In the "Going to the Movies" section, we examine the individual films. As a film is presented, its title appears, along with the name of its director, its country of origin (if outside the United States), the year it was first released, its running time, and the MPAA (Motion Picture Association of America) rating. The "Plot" section provides a brief overview of the major characters and events of the movie. "Reflections" offers an analysis of the film and its relation to the major theme. Following this section are discussion/reflection questions for both individual and group use. At the end of the book you will find a guide for leading a film study group; a list of additional films for study, organized by major theme; notes, organized by chapter; and a glossary of film terms used in the book.

Note: All motion pictures are protected by copyright law. Before showing or viewing any movie, whether individually or with a group, please review carefully "The Fine Print" (found in the back of the book) for a briefing of the applicable copyright law and a related list of frequently asked questions and answers.

This is a strange book, as all books on movies must be, by their very nature. Either you have seen a film before you read the discussion of it, or you have not. If you have not seen the film, I don't want to spoil your pleasure in a first viewing by giving away all the surprises. If you have, you are in a better position to read the film's analysis, because then you will be able to dispute my findings and add your own observations.

I have a chosen a middle path—one that guides without explaining away all of the "magic." In part 1, "Home," I offer a fresh and independent voice in filmmaking—Cynthia Scott—who challenges many of the assumptions of Hollywood storytelling (such as that all movies must have conflict, major stars, and a rapid pace) and in chapter 1 we will examine *Strangers in Good Company.* In part 2, "The Journey," the discussion is organized around signposts along life's journey, using films that highlight issues in particularly intriguing ways. Each analysis is designed to be suggestive rather than exhaustive, providing points of entry for further discussion. Each chapter in this section pairs contemporary American films with films from other countries or with "classic" films from an earlier period. Part 3, "Healing," pulls together the various perspectives in part 2 through an analysis of the beautiful but problematic *The English Patient.*

All of the films in this book have been chosen because they take life from the search for the deeper meanings that lie behind life's surface events and seemingly chance encounters. In all of the films, restorative love is affirmed—sometimes at great price—against attempts to devalue human life. Together, all of the chapters in this book provide an arena for theological reflection, from creation through journey and healing to celebration—the familiar pattern of Christian redemption and salvation. The discussions are not limited to a Christian paradigm, however. Judaism is the source for the metaphors, parables, and stories that animate the Christian faith. We are a covenant people who have strayed into the far country; we are sons and daughters of a waiting father or mother; we have been brought out of bondage into freedom. We long for righteousness and purity of heart, the songs of the Psalms. These metaphors of righteousness and purity still live for us, even if in our daily lives we sometimes forget the biblical names and faces.

The majority of the films we will consider are contemporary. But I could hardly offer a book that proposes to move between theology and film without including a few works of artists who consciously tried to express religious convictions or quests through film: Ingmar Bergman, Andrei Tarkovsky, and Robert Bresson. There was a time in the United States when only a privileged few could see the gems that came out of the thriving movie industries of Sweden, Denmark, Japan, India, France, and Germany. "Art houses" flourished during the 1960s, but they largely disappeared during the 1970s and 1980s as the large Hollywood studios became more dominant. Even now, American viewers have access to only a small percentage of the films that come out of France or Germany, and almost no access to films from even the largest film companies in the Chinas, Iran, India, and Egypt. The movie fan who lives in Chicago, New York, or Los Angeles is fortunate since international films are often shown there. Recently, however, owners of cineplexes in other cities began to include independent films on their lists. And because distribution companies now understand how much money can be earned through video rentals worldwide, hundreds of film treasures from outside the U.S. are as close as your nearest library lending service or video store.

Most foreign films shown in the U.S. feature subtitles. In viewing subtitled films, a few cautions are in order. While persons who are hard of hearing may appreciate movies with written text on the screen, others may find watching films with subtitles a bit taxing. Viewing them on a large-screen television helps, as does providing a brief plot/character summary for the group to read before the film is shown—a technique used by cinema clubs in other countries before they watch American films.

Why include classic films or foreign films at all? Why not stick only to movies that come to the local cineplex? In theory, we could initiate good discussions about serious issues by using any movie, even by using a television commercial. We could examine the premises (underlying ideas), coding (e.g., key words or colors), or marketing strategies for the commercial, or even some advertisers' practice of depicting the customer not as a consumer but as a dreamer. We could limit our film discussions to movies produced for mass consumption within the last twelve months, or even to films released just last summer. There have been and will be great movies among the thousands produced to make money for major studios; as Tom Gunning has said, some of the greatest movies ever made were made for mass consumption.[1]

I include classic and non-American films because I want to stretch our awareness of cinema's storytelling possibilities. The films I have chosen present ways to explore the human condition that may be new and surprising to American viewers. The maker of these films—like the makers of the other films in this book—were and are artists who had a vision of what it meant to search the self and stand with others under God. They marshaled their gifts of storytelling to share those understandings with us. For those writers and directors who consider art the most precious expression of human gifts, we pay them homage to visit and revisit their storied worlds.

Acknowledgments

Readers familiar with the growing literature on religion and film will recognize my debt to such pioneers in the analysis of American film as John Cawelti, John R. May, and Robert Jewett. Books by Margaret Miles and Martha Nussbaum have motivated me to reflect anew on the public function of drama and film. Jeffrey Mahan introduced me to the delights of attending to the messages of popular culture. Tom Gunning's work on silent film (along with his cheerful friendship) continues to inspire my research and writing.

Grateful thanks to Sarah, Catherine, Bert, and Keith Vaux; Mary Lofton; Holly Hudnut Halliday; Milt Nieuswma; Jan and Catherine van Eys; Barbara DeCoster; Cathy Rafferty; Richard Kieckhefer; and Robert Jewett for their assistance.

Robert L. Patten, superb teacher and loving mentor, first encouraged me to think and to write. My husband, Ken, and my children continue to keep me anchored in the real world.

Sara Anson Vaux

Introduction

> ## "Deserve's got nothin' to do with it."
>
> *Will Munny, as he prepares to kill corrupt sheriff Little Bill, in* Unforgiven

In the 1992 film *Unforgiven*, William Munny, an aging former gunfighter, has begun to try his hand at farming, influenced by the memory of his wife Claudia (who died some years before the movie begins). Will and his former partner, Ned, have both abandoned their violent lives, but Will, his farm failing, undertakes one last bounty hunt to secure money to feed his children. Ned joins him out of loyalty and affection.

Neither Will nor Ned shows any appetite for their assigned task: hunting down two men who mutilated a young prostitute. Only Ned's death—wrongfully visited on an innocent man who had begun to turn home to his wife—ignites Will's old violent fury, and in an explosion of gunfire, he executes Ned's killer and all who surround him.

Exaction of justice by a hero has provided a bare-bones plot for many movies over the near-century of the Western. However, *Unforgiven* appeared in 1992, long after the Western had faded as a popular movie genre. Further, its portrait of Will Munny, the protagonist, is not that of a blameless hero or even a seamless villain, but one of a deeply conflicted person, just like most of us, who struggles with the need to carry his religious convictions over into his everyday world of work and family. At the beginning of the movie, not only does Will clearly believe that his former sins have been forgiven, he also realizes that he needs to continue to ask that forgiveness. By movie's end, his riding off in a dark and merciless downpour may signal both *despair* over his (necessary and inescapable) fall and *hope* that he can be baptized into new life. The question of "deserving"— whether either suffering or prosperity is connected with mortal virtue or purity—recalls the insistent debunking of easy answers about life and death in the book of Job.

The western can provide a way to reexamine America's past—particularly its rocky history of slavery, civil war, and extermination of native peoples—and to suggest that both individuals and social groups can reject violence and alienation in favor of peace and cooperation. *The Outlaw Josey Wales* (1976), also starring Eastwood, did this. *Unforgiven* calls up *Wales's* respect for the vulnerable and rejected of our booming American nation, while it infuses the movie with the most radical questions of religious faith: Can we indeed choose life over death? What resources do we have within the differing domains of friendship, faith, and family to do this? How completely do we believe Jesus' radical message of forgiveness, that even the worst person can be forgiven?

Movies such as *Unforgiven* may offer the most compelling places today to raise questions of religion and value. They provide us with a fantasy arena where we can test situations and relationships that in ordinary life we may be too preoccupied or timid or frightened to think through; movies also provide us with safe boundaries, as John Cawelti has observed.[1] But most critically, they stimulate us to imagine how we can translate our own beliefs and values from the protected shelter of our places of worship out into the worlds of chance and choice. Movies, when they encourage this kind of reflection, can be part of our ongoing worship life.

In theory, any movie could be used to launch discussions about meaning and value. In practice, narrative films — movies that tell stories — work best, because stories provide points of entry for our own spiritual and moral pilgrimage. The movies I have chosen to discuss in this book are distinguished by the particularly powerful ways in which they use the resources of film language to tell their stories.

Almost all of the films in this book lack an easily recognized "religious" subject, though several include pastors among their characters. To be sure, biblical stories have supplied cinema with countless plots over the past century. But as it is human existence itself in its mystery and drama that continues to give life to religious texts, the meatiest religious material is often that which is lifted off our daily plate.[2] After all, the Bible itself is not only the account of God's search for a home on earth with people, but also a weave of narratives telling the stories of people who search for meaning in their lives and seek to embody that meaning in the world. Our appetite to tell our own stories — and our eagerness to digest the tales our appointed creators of myth and artifice (writers, filmmakers) tell about us and for us — reveal how hungry we are to voice our life's concerns.

The ways in which stories are told — their artistic form — may determine whether these concerns are well or poorly satisfied. Although any film could be used to stimulate discussion, those that have been thoughtfully conceived and well crafted retain their power to disturb or enlighten long after other films have come and gone. There is a great deal of difference between a movie that reinforces all our old prejudices and allows us to hide inside our personally designed comfort zones, and the disturbing (and beautiful) *Sling Blade* or *Blade Runner* or *Secrets & Lies*. For story not only *relates* experience, it also *gives shape* to it, and its shape affects the way we viewers understand that experience. We are as eager to understand the dimensions of our daily lives as others are to play with the plots that our lives provide for them.

If we are to probe the meanings and understand the ethical issues that surface in movies, we must look at the ways in which those movies present their stories and offer their information. For instance, the great communal dinners in *Antoina's Line* (1995), *Secrets & Lies* (1996), and *Sling Blade* (1996) are all photographed with great care. These family dinners represent the communion table, where outsiders are brought into the fellowship of love and all can put down their burdens and open their hearts.

If simply exciting and pleasing the audience and making money are the primary goals of moviemaking, then we need to be alert when we view even the most highly praised movies. The great push of Hollywood cinema, as Margaret Miles and others have pointed out, is toward convention and conformity—providing a happy ending; portraying disaster overcome without pain; or glossing over potentially disrupting issues such as racism, religious nonconformity, women's concerns, and the legacy of colonization, to note a few examples. At the same time, the level of screen violence and explicit sexual activity has escalated, frequently unmotivated by the requirements of plot logic. As viewers, we must ask ourselves: Are our emotions being manipulated? Are tough issues being raised only to be sugared over? Are we settling for boring plots or movies with no story at all? Are our beliefs and attitudes being challenged in creative ways, or are they being ignored in favor of "popcorn and candy for the mind"?[3]

Being a discerning viewer of movies must be part, then, of an overall plan of watching and discussing them. One can hardly exist without the other. What you hear in a film may be completely undercut by what you see on the screen. Discussions about class, wealth, loyalty, love, or family ties take on different colors depending on the film in which they occur—as in, for example, *The Godfather, Steel Magnolias, Boyz N the Hood*, or *Daughters of the Dust*. You must enter the total world of the movie and understand the speakers' words in the context in which they appear. It is misleading to discuss themes apart from the *form* they appear in. Meaning, as Kristin Thompson has written, is only one of the parts of a work of art.[4] Similarly, it would be idle to analyze a movie's story structure, imagery, or symbol system without engaging with the themes and issues that make it worth watching at all.

We are about to explore a group of movies whose common denominators are their quality—their quality as *films* rather than as some other kind of work—and their power to raise questions of meaning and value. These films have been organized in a particular way: by their most prominent (but by no means their only) theological theme. In each case I have also highlighted some other feature that sets the film apart as unusual and enriches its meanings: for example, in both *Secrets & Lies* and *Strangers in Good Company,* the use of photographs to tell different kinds of stories; in *Lone Star* and *Unforgiven,* particularly complex and searching narratives; in *Daughters of the Dust,* creative use of music, games, and color; in *Solaris,* long, deliberate "takes" (scenes without a cut); and so forth. Again, I must caution against reducing such wonderful movies as these to a sum of their themes or ideas. Their integrity as individual works of art should be respected.

Nonetheless, I find that examining each film with a focus such as "alienation" or "celebration" allows us to connect with its creator's seriousness of purpose and also permits us to organize the complex perceptions a great movie provokes. One friend of mine particularly delights in the classic Italian movie *The Tree of the Wooden Clogs,* finding a central theme, the dignity of the common life, a compelling one.[5] Driving his admiration for this film is his sense of the director's dominant intent: to respect the aspirations of each one of us, poor or titled. The director's respect for his subjects has determined his choice of actors (largely unknown), camera distance and focus (long and medium shots, little distortion), pace (rather slow, allowing events to unfold), and narrative style (episodic) would be used.

Without irony or condescension, he also allows his characters to voice and demonstrate their deep religious faith.

Another friend adores a completely different kind of movie, *Blade Runner,* finding its frequent and daring uses of religious symbolism (which are often in conflict with what we see and hear in the movie's story) a source of endless fascination.[6] For instance, what colors did the director use in this movie? Steel blues and washed yellows, no hint of earth tones, since *Blade Runner* is a movie set in a technologically advanced, morally misshapen society.

Part One: HOME

SCENE: 1
TAKE: 1

HOME

Strangers in Good Company

INTRODUCTION

> *"Toto, we're home. . . . There's no place like home."*
>
> *Dorothy, in*
> The Wizard of Oz

Home for Dorothy and Toto, we all recognize, was Kansas—the heartland of America—not the dream (or nightmare) world of wicked witches, red slippers, and a tin man. The magical transformations in *The Wizard of Oz* were created by light and mirrors—little men hiding behind curtains, pulling strings, engineering the illusion of the movies. Dorothy's Technicolor frolics were dreamtime trips into her imagination, gifting her with a new appreciation of the beauties of the land and people who made up her daytime "real life."

Oz is a charmer. It makes me love the Midwest and my own past as much as I love Iowa and baseball each time I see *Field of Dreams*. It praises the normalcy of a certain time and age, while secretly stepping over the line into another dimension — a zone that liberates thought, expands horizons, and stimulates the better self.

"Home" is a potent cultural idea; the Polish director Krzysztof Kieslowski once said that the longing for home is the most enduring theme in storytelling.[1] Born of the human instinct to nest and to shelter, it travels with the gypsies or the Bedouins (as shown in *Latcho Drom* and *The English Patient*) or burrows in for settled generations. No place on earth is exempt from its mythmaking potential; if Poland and the Balkans represent parts of the world torn by repeated disruptions of war and by boundary shifts, America's history is one of displaced persons seeking some spot on which to pitch a tent and begin a new life, undisturbed. The idea of home calls forth a powerful, protective response: the hearth, warmth, a place of refuge.

The movie that made Kieslowski internationally famous, *The Double Life of Veronica*, is not unlike *The Wizard of Oz*: In each, the filmmaker explores the meaning of a person's life against a dreamlike background. In this case, the life of a young French woman, Veronica, is compared with that of her double, a Polish singer who dies at a young age. Veronica is sucked into a world where she begins to lose sight of her own history and identity. As the movie ends, Veronica rushes up the sidewalk of a modest house, where an older man waits with open arms. She is home — not only safe, but centered.[2]

European moviegoers would have recognized the similarity of this finale to the final scene between astronaut Kris Kelvin and his father in *Solaris*, Andrei Tarkovsky's great film from 1972. In *Solaris*, Kris, psychologist and space traveler, returns home not only to embrace his father but to fall at his feet, arms locked around his knees.[3] Kris comes to himself like the prodigal son, his past not only recognized, but relived.

Home for Kris, as for Veronica, means laying down the burdens of confusion and moving into a redeemed, *kairos* time, the sacred space that Ellie, the scientist in *Contact,* enters—a place where affections are renewed and mysteries are acknowledged. Home, wherever it is physically located, is represented in the Bible as stability—a stable—"an atmosphere to shape living and behaving," the human shape of the divine journey into our lives.[4]

> He came down to earth from heaven
> Who is God and Lord of all,
> And his shelter was a stable,
> And his cradle was a stall.
> With the poor, the scorned, the lowly,
> Lived on earth our Savior holy.
> (hymn, "Once in Royal David's City")

Home is stability but not stagnation. It is our good earth, home to us all regardless of gender, class, age, or ethnicity— the *oikos,* life not only as viable but valuable.[5]

Strangers in Good Company explores these theological dimensions of home in a quiet way: no trip to Oz, no trip to Vega— simply an afternoon's drive out into the countryside, with a busload of elderly women searching for an abandoned farmhouse.[6] As surely as in *Contact, Veronica,* or *Solaris,* home in this film is also a place of comfort and belonging, generator of the storehouse of memories and values we draw on to sustain our daily lives. It's a Kingdom place—like the household to which the prodigal son returns; like God's house with "many rooms" (John 14:2 NIV).

I have chosen to begin with *Strangers in Good Company* not only because this film explores the idea of home as a place of centering and spiritual growth, but also because it presents its story with a style that quietly challenges many Hollywood storytelling conventions. Although it never falters from its mission to tell the world about the marvelous adventures of its heroines, it does so not with bursts of action punctuated by gunfire, but by taking its time, often almost silently. The effect is stimulating and haunting. The film's central idea is the same as that of the classic *Wild Strawberries*—that a person can be born into new life at any age. But I have saved *Strawberries* for later. Let's savor for the moment the sweetness of life-changing journeys for seven older women.

GOING TO THE MOVIES

Strangers in Good Company
Cynthia Scott, Canada, 1990, 101 min.; PG

This modest film made no major splash in the movie market when it appeared in 1990.[7] Shot on a small budget by Canadian documentary filmmaker Cynthia Scott, it was not designed to compete with summer blockbusters in either the Unites States or the rest of the media-hungry world. However, among film lovers, religious groups, and young professionals, the appeal of its stunning cinematography and low-key narrative style has captured a growing audience.

Strangers presents a world whose beauty is rooted in its sense of the wholeness and worth of all life. Its surface tale, its story, embraces the search for the meaning of life that has motivated the telling of stories in countless generations and cultures past.[8] In many ways *Strangers* resembles *Daughters of the Dust* (see chapter 7, "Celebration"). It respects age and aging, and it lovingly relates the stories of women without slighting men. Its tone is one of both elegy and celebration—elegy for lost times and places, but also celebration of life's ever-renewing possibilities.[9] These possibilities include the power of storytelling to elevate the experiences of ordinary people and to fashion from their hopes and tales a world in which rebirth is accepted and welcomed at any time of life. The movie is built on the real-life experiences of the women who appear in the film, but it reaches far beyond documentary into the worlds of myth and dream.

PLOT Seven elderly women and their bus driver, Michelle, out for an afternoon's excursion, take a detour down a country lane to visit the childhood home of Constance, a rather depressed octogenarian. The bus unexpectedly breaks down far from the nearest town. The only hardy one among them, the young driver, sprains her ankle. The women hobble to a deserted house they spy far off the road, where they are forced to scratch for food and shelter for the night. They are rescued after several days, thanks to Catherine, a nun with arthritic feet, who hikes twenty miles to get help.

REFLECTIONS The action that initiates the film is the search for "home." Quite literally, Constance wants to see the place where she had spent happy summers some eighty years ago. When the group nears the house, she frets, "That's not it," but it is too late to turn back. They have been stranded. As all of the women are somewhat limited physically and most live alone, it is possible that no one will miss them for a week or longer. They are totally without resources to survive, and, moreover, most depend heavily on their local pharmacies to keep them alive.

How can the filmmaker capture the attention of an audience accustomed to conflict- and action-driven movies?[10] *Strangers* is off to an unconventional start: There are no stars, and only one woman, Michelle, has youth and beauty—the qualities savored by Hollywood films. But although Michelle gets to showcase her vibrant jazz singing and rich conversational style, the camera does not focus uniquely on her. It lingers instead on the collapsing farmhouse, the surface of the lake, and the changing colors of the sky. The narrative style of the movie "respects long silences and pays attention to small details."[11] There are long sections of quiet punctuated only by bird calls and crickets' chirps.[12]

Oddly, there seems to be no conflict in this film at all—not even the one we expect: the race against time. We expect time to provide an organizing structure for this film. (Will the women be rescued before their medications give out?) But it doesn't.[13] Quite the contrary. Instead, time seems to vanish. Even the appearance of "set" shots of the house taken at different times of day, which might tempt us to measure time's passing by the rising or setting of the sun, doesn't work as a marker of time.

But *chronos* (clock-driven) time is not the point of this movie. We are meant to move into *kairos* (Kingdom) time, where words such as *age* or *success* or *worth* receive a serious reworking. These women have stepped away from a culture that values above all youth, beauty, money, and time, into a timeless place where relationship, memory, and self-affirmation take precedence.

How does the film prepare us to change our perspective? In the opening sequence, the director first blurs what we think we see.[14] She has made careful choices about visual style. Instead of crisp, focused images of people moving actively toward some goal, we see a white and cloudy screen. As the fog begins to lift, we dimly spy a line of women walking, but we're not sure where they are going or who they are. Gradually we're aware of another image coming up behind this one. The women appear to be walking on the tops of trees, or maybe through the treetops. Anything can happen.[15]

A dreamy narrative voice begins to speak, telling us that Constance wants to visit her long-lost home.[16] But soon this voice disappears, and we are on our own.

The women assess their situation: food supplies, pills, shelter. They talk of escape. So far, we are anchored in the present time. When night comes, however, the narrative moves into a new consciousness. This shift is accomplished by carefully framing the women in groups, often together. The use of shot/counter shot (one person is talking, then the camera switches to the face of the other to show reaction and response) is a common convention of movie storytelling. It can be manipulated to give greater weight to one person's words over the other or to show that the two people are equal in importance.

By contrast, the women in *Strangers* are usually shown in the same frame, in conversation but not in competition. There are few close-ups and few shots of one person alone (Constance being a notable exception). The camera moves among the women, peeping in on almost-sleeping pairs and eavesdropping on what appear to be quite unstaged conversations.[17]

The women's conversations gradually move us away from the present time back into memory. They begin to share stories: Cissy has made a miraculous comeback from a stroke. Mary came out as a lesbian when she was about sixty. Beth's only son died, and after forty years, she is still grieving. Each time the camera shifts its attentive focus, we discover more secrets about these women's lives. The tales are linked not so much by revelation or connection but by each woman's interest in the stories of the others. The episodes of everyday life unfold with quiet dignity.

By this time in the film, we have grown comfortable with our role as private witnesses to real life. Suddenly, not only do we hear about Cissy's past life though her conversation with Mary, but we also are shown photographs of her as a child, a hopeful young girl, and a blossoming young woman. No dialogue or voice-over explains the photographs. The photos themselves become part of the narrative: We must create the story from our imagination. We ourselves begin to fill in the missing background *(fabula)* information. For instance, what energy and determination did it take for Mary to enter the armed services fifty years ago? What happened to turn Catherine toward a career in the church? What other career possibilities were open to women in the 1930s and 1940s? How did World War II affect their lives?

We are familiar with one variation of this technique from written stories, the *flashback* —the storytelling device that provides a shortcut to "Once upon a time" or "Do you remember when?"[18] Photos can provide a shortcut in storytelling, a way of telling the tale without dialogue, as when the hero (Clint Eastwood) in *Absolute Power* picks up a photo of himself with a young child. This simple action not only primes us to meet his daughter, it also tells us that his relationship with her is one filled with regret and longing. The use of photos in *Strangers* is different. Four or five photos are shown for each woman (except Michelle) —without commentary, not rushed, giving full time for us, the viewers, to fill in each woman's history.

What a contrast with normal movie storytelling! In conventional Hollywood editing, every attempt is made to create and maintain the illusion of reality. Cuts are made to provide eyeline matches and match on action; music binds shots within a sequence.[19] We are meant to think that the action we see before us on the screen represents the small part of life we might see through a videocamera lens or through a window if we were standing on tiptoe looking into a room. We are led to believe that the rest of the world around that scene actually exists, waiting for us to turn our heads to notice it.

So convincing is this style of editing (called *continuity editing*) that it takes some effort to remember that all movies are created works of art rather than windows to events that are actually happening before us. That wall in front of us in the theater is a flat surface with thousands of little dots on it, not a magic mirror we can walk through —as much as we might wish to!

Strangers doesn't seem interested in creating a magical world. It respects the history of each individual woman — her experiences and the dreams that shaped her life. In a youth and money culture, people who are elderly or who are poor, particularly women, are often disregarded. Even wealthy, accomplished women are overlooked as they grow older. Their fragility and vulnerability is voiced by the evil queen's mirror in *Snow White:* The mirror gives us the sure and deadly reminder that we all decay and die.

Most of the women in *Strangers* feel this neglect keenly. In the past, most of them have received affirmation from their husbands or children, or even from a job. But now, husbands have died, children have passed into busy lives or may have died, and jobs are gone. What's left? "I had a small talent that I didn't develop," Constance laments. She stopped nourishing it when she married and threw herself into child rearing and housework, and now she thinks it is too late to reclaim that past pleasure. This makes her doubly vulnerable.

Can Constance revive her talent? Can any of these women regain the hope that lit their days when they were young? This is the question Nicodemus urgently asked Jesus some two thousand years ago: "How can anyone be born after having grown old?" (John 3:4 NRSV). The photographs that accompany these women's stories provide illustrated histories of lives, but they also give us a visual way to ask Nicodemus's question.

The search for Constance's childhood home is understood by some of the other women to stand for Constance's fear of death: "She seems so unhappy." Perhaps the home she seeks is not a physical location or a place after death, but new birth in the present.

Significantly, the first of the photographs is shown after the moving exchange between Mary and Cissy (discussed above), when Mary tells Sissy her experience of "coming out" about her sexuality. Cissy, herself a recovered victim of stroke, is free to appreciate Mary's worth. Mary responds by drawing out the drama of Cissy's own life—her recovery from near death and disability: "You're a miracle." Mary and Cissy have already begun journeys toward new birth.

For the other women, the journeys toward home commence when they start taking action to feed themselves—when they stop thinking of life as only what they know and begin to imagine what it might become. Their terrors are real: loneliness; fear that their children will die before them; fear of becoming destitute. Constance voices the concern all feel: "I'd rather die here than in a nursing home or hospital." "I'm not going to die," retorts a listening Alice, "I'm going fishing." This is the plot turn that the Greeks called the *peripeteia*—a sudden change of events or reversal of circumstances—but it also marks a shift toward *metanoia*—change of heart—for all the women.[20]

The most vivid metaphor for new birth swirls around the bird songs, which create a sense of the isolation of the old house in which the women find themselves and a feeling for the natural beauty of its surroundings. New birth involves new ways of seeing, as Cissy and Mary track the birds with their binoculars. It also captures new ways of hearing; Constance, who has returned to the scene of long-vanished happiness with the memory of those birds' calls in her mind, is no longer physically capable of hearing them. The patient and attentive Mary gently coaxes her to remember the songs she once heard. Suddenly, Constance purses her lips and makes the sound herself. This marks her move forward into an active life.[21]

One of the key sequences in the film occurs outside around an old car, when a discussion about "young people today" turns toward the women themselves. Is it possible to fall in love again? Yes! Love is affirmed not only for the young, but for each one of *them,* as well. Instead of thinking of home as a physical place, our women have begun to create a new home through the stories they tell one another.[22] This is indeed a new place, a recovery of and movement toward home as the kingdom of God—time out of time. For as Jesus says in Luke 17:21, "In fact, the kingdom of God is among you" (NRSV).

QUESTIONS 1. Vocation or "calling" is important in this film. Catherine, the nun, tells Michelle that you discover your calling through prayer. How do her words find expression in her actions? How does the movie explore the idea of calling? Is hers the only true calling?

2. Late in the film, Constance stands alone on the porch where she has often sat, mourning her lost life. Suddenly she opens her pill bottle and dumps the pills out. How can you explain this act? Can the movie support differing interpretations? At what points, and how?

3. Constance takes her first steps out of the protection of the group when she walks toward the boathouse. This scene is divided into at least thirteen separate shots. There is no dialogue. Suddenly, we see her across the lake at the boathouse. We don't know how she has gotten there in her frail condition. What effect does the absence of sound and the missing scene *(ellipsis)* have on our reading of Constance's thoughts at this stage? How might this episode have been filmed differently?

4. Jesus teaches about the heavenly kingdom or the kingdom of God. In the Sermon on the Mount (Matthew 5:1–7:29), he gives a specific description of this kingdom. Where in the film are aspects of Jesus' kingdom revealed?

5. The past history of seven of the women is told through photographs. Only Michelle is omitted. What role does this young woman play in the drama of the older women? Why has her story been excluded? Does this omission tighten or damage the overall story?

6. Many narrative movies present clear conflicts between good and evil. What does this film gain by avoiding such a sharp contrast? Is evil absent altogether from the world of this movie?

7. What do you learn from the movie about women's lives (working conditions, attitudes toward women in the society in general, child rearing, vocational choice, and conditions that enhance or destroy self-esteem)?

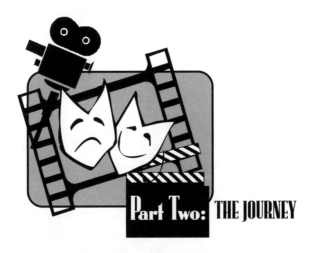

Part Two: THE JOURNEY

INTRODUCTION

The chapters on home and healing in parts 1 and 3 offer films of unusual suggestiveness and beauty. We have seen how the quiet, contemplative style of *Strangers in Good Company* encourages us to reconsider the possibility of new birth. Although *The English Patient* has a far more dramatic style, youth, wealth, and social position deliver no protections against war or accident. The characters in *Patient* find themselves as bereft of hope as the women in *Strangers* were when they arrived, tired and hungry, at the isolated farmhouse at the beginning of that film.

The "English" patient is burned beyond recognition. The woman who nurses him is scarred in her heart from war; she sees death. For these persons and for the others whose stories are bound up with theirs, the movement from death to life may resemble limping through the wilderness on swollen feet, cursing the shortness of the day and the certainty of death. Yet it also can take strength from the earth's beauty and the mysterious and irresistible appearances of human affection. The journey can become the way toward transformation, toward opening the heart to be healed. To imitate a bird's call—to dance in a sick room—to respond to a call for help, when you yourself need rescue—these are actions that defy time, logic, and the seductions of despair.

The films in parts 1 and 3 are discussed in their entirety, film diaries that examine a world in need of healing from many perspectives. The movies in part 2 stop at different signposts along life's journey to explore particular dimensions of human existence. The places where pain and loss are felt most severely may lie within the walls of the household, as in *Cries and Whispers* and *Secrets & Lies;* they may be felt as cosmic disorder, as in *Contact* and *Blade Runner.* The individual person may struggle to construct a meaningful set of values outside a community of faith, as in *Lone Star* and *Unforgiven.* A religious vocation or a job may be used as a prop to give life a sense of purpose, as in *Diary of a Country Priest* or *Wall Street.* Healers within a broken world may not be persons of power or magic, but rather fools or outcasts *(La Strada* and *Sling Blade),* or older women *(Babette's Feast)* or the marginalized *(Daughters of the Dust; Ulee's Gold).* The films in the final chapters of part 2 move steadily toward celebration, a time and place of reconciliation and rejoicing—expressions of the wholeness for which all characters have yearned.

Sin follows closely upon creation, or, in other tellings of the ancient story, was born a part of it. The discomfort, even misery, common to the characters in Cries and Whispers *and in* Secrets & Lies *comes from an acute consciousness that somehow the ways they are living their lives "miss the mark"—one way of translating the New Testament word for sin,* hamartia. *The human being is a creature who worries, André Le Cocque has written. Karin in* Cries *is consumed by guilt; Cynthia and Monica in* Secrets *sit alone on their stairways, remembering the past. Somehow, the search for the authentic self cannot begin until a person acknowledges that something has gone terribly wrong. In* Cries, *the vision of wholeness may be available only to the pure in heart, such as the maid Anna, or to the spectator of the film. In* Secrets, *the authentic life is born out of painful truth-telling and is sealed in garden celebration.*

SCENE: **2**
TAKE:

AUTHENTICITY

Cries and Whispers
Secrets & Lies

INTRODUCTION

> "*Here I am with my mother.*"
>
> *Rachael in* Blade Runner *showing a photo to Deckard, who suspects she is not human.*

In Andrei Tarkovsky's *Solaris* and Ridley Scott's *Blade Runner,* the heroines suffer a severe crisis of identity. Not only does Hari of *Solaris* not know where home is, she can't even remember what her own face looks like. In anguish, Rachael of *Blade Runner* holds up photographs of herself as a child to prove to bounty hunter Rick Deckard that she is an authentic person, not a phony or manufactured one.

The dilemmas of these women cut deeper than simply fretting about themselves as image or icon (a problem Princess Diana is said to have struggled with). The question is, Who am I *inside* that is separate from the identities everyone projects on me? As we will explore in the next chapter, Hari and Rachael are creations not of a loving God who validates that unique identity, but rather products of memories and madness—Hari, a projection of her husband's guilty memories of her, and Rachael, a creation of Tyrell Corporation (Los Angeles, A.D. 2019) as part of a massive experiment in human genetics.

Solaris and *Blade Runner* grapple not only with the potential evils of human experimentation—the drive toward perfection without regard for consequences—but also with the spiritual dimension of the personality. Hari and Rachael want to know who they are not so much by *name* as by *relation,* connecting with others and before God.

"Who am I"—the search for an authentic self—means equally "whose am I," the cry of Augustine. "I was admonished . . . to return to my own self, and, with you to guide me, I entered into the innermost part of myself, and I was able to do this because you were my helper."[1] As Calvin wrote, "Without knowledge of self there is no knowledge of God. . . . No one can look upon himself without immediately turning his thoughts to the contemplation of God, in whom he 'lives and moves.' . . . The mighty gifts with which we are endowed are hardly from ourselves; indeed, our very being is nothing but subsistence in the one God."[2]

Likewise, "Without knowledge of God there is no knowledge of self." Calvin wrote very much to the point of authenticity: "For, because all of us are inclined by nature to hypocrisy, a kind of empty image of righteousness in place of righteousness itself abundantly satisfies us."[3] The biblical

blessed those

grounding is unmistakable: "Keep the commandments. . . . Sell your possessions" (Matthew 19:17, 21 NRSV). "You shall love your neighbor as yourself" (Matthew 19:19 NRSV). Without the love of self, love of God and love of neighbor cannot flourish; without love of God and service to the neighbor, the self is lost. To know the truth allows us to stand face to face—before God and with one another, without masks or pretensions.

REFLECTIONS "I don't know who I am" is the first step toward authenticity. Not fabricated images, but real persons in touch with truth and linked with one another—this is the kind of knowledge that the characters in *Cries and Whispers* and *Secrets & Lies* crave. Their hoarded memories are shrouds stitched over anxious bodies and fretful minds to block them off from other persons, even their closest family members. The identity of the self may be well hidden within the tangle of family relationships, where secrets and lies may take on particularly strange and vicious shapes. In the movies that follow, the search for truth proceeds within that dangerous human community called *family*, in which relationships may be tainted by years—even generations—of carefully guarded secrets and lies.[4]

GOING TO THE MOVIES

Cries and Whispers
Ingmar Bergman, Sweden, 1972, 91 min.; Not Rated

 This profoundly moving film can be read in many ways: as a judgment on the shallowness of lives dominated by wealth and appearances; as the history of sisters within a dysfunctional family; as a psychological drama; or as a portrayal of the anguish of dying and death. The unmistakably religious character of the movie infuses each of these levels but also transcends them. At the movie's center, for instance, lies Agnes's suffering and death. Death is presented not as the peaceful slipping away into the night seen in so many films; it is, for Agnes, a slow and excruciating agony of unbearable pain.

PLOT Maria and Karin have returned to their ancestral home to await the death of their sister Agnes. Both have married, neither happily. Flashbacks reflect their inner desires: Maria remembers a past affair with the local doctor, as well as the consequent suicide attempt of her husband; Karin remembers (or fantasizes about) an icy meal with her aged and imperious husband, after which she defiantly broke her wine glass and used a piece of it to cut her vagina.

Karin wants to connect with Maria. Sadly, Maria, as her lover once told her, exists only as an image or projection before others and may have no interior life. But Agnes's hideous agony, which alternates with her grateful reception of her sisters' touch (they bathe and feed her), could become an instrument by which the reconciliation of Karin and Maria is brought about.

Agnes dies. The sisters dismiss Anna, Agnes's longtime nurse and companion. The film ends as Anna reads Agnes's precious diary.

REFLECTIONS After Agnes's death, her story is not over. Her corpse calls to each of her sisters, then to her friend Anna, in an appeal that echoes the idea expressed in Matthew 25, verses 31-46: Show your love not by words, but by acts. From beyond death, Agnes speaks, "Hold me. I'm cold." Anna's faithful response to that call—she cradles the corpse against her breast in death as she had cradled Agnes in sickness—reflects the allegiance of the faithful servant, lowly in this life but elevated in the kingdom of God. She is the righteous one, the person who knows and practices *heʃeð* — steadfast love, loyalty, and faithfulness. Righteousness is service; it is relationship; it is acts of kindness that issue from a life of faith. The Sermon on the Mount, set within an expansive vision of the kingdom of God, includes those who "hunger and thirst for righteousness" (Matthew 5:6 NRSV). Anna is whole in faith and whole in self. Anna's life, quiet and ordinary, is the one to watch in this film, for it grounds the search for authenticity in faith, not in reason or psychology.

Nonetheless, secrets swirl around Anna. Who fathered her child? Who were her parents? What was her relation to Agnes? How can Agnes's sisters dismiss Anna so crassly, when (we assume) she has lived with them all her life? Where did Anna learn to read? How has she developed and sustained her strong faith? Little background information is revealed about her, and the questions remain.

One reason they remain is the garish nature of the sisters' secrets. Agnes's physical suffering is intensified by her memories of a loveless childhood. Questions are also raised about her mother and father, for she is deeply wounded. Further, Agnes did not marry, even though the family's wealth would have made this possible, even obligatory. At Agnes's death service, the pastor speaks of her great faith; does it sustain her through her suffering?

Agnes's approaching death stimulates self-reflection, a return to the well of ancient memories — not only for her, but for her sisters. Karin and Maria are granted rare time to reflect and refresh — to look into the mirror and see beyond their surface glamour, wealth, and image; to penetrate the "tissue of lies" that consumes Karin with "all that guilt."

Agnes's death is presented in the movie, then, as offering an opening for all the sisters to tear down the walls that years and phoniness have set between them and to stand face to face (see 1 Corinthians 13:12). What does Karin's guilt refer to: Karin's hatred for her husband's infidelities? Theft? The origins of the family's wealth? Or lost faith? The honesty that the intrusion of a death in the family can provoke offers a chance to ask those difficult questions and face the answers.

The movie presents (among others) three defining moments where issues of authenticity could be explored: the pastor's sermon; the near-reconciliation between Maria and Karin; and the closing sequence of the film, where we hear Agnes's voice as Anna reads her diary.

The pastor begins simply, standing in the shadows beside Agnes's bed, framed against a red wall. "God has called you home in the flower of your youth. Prior to that, he found you *worthy* to bear a heavy and prolonged suffering. . . . May he let his angels disrobe you of the memory of your earthly pain."[5] This is traditional language about separation of the suffering of the body and the release of the soul—very Pauline, very Greek, but not helpful to those who need peace for the whole self.

Slowly, almost mechanically, the pastor now moves into the light of the window and kneels by Agnes's bedside in the position of a suppliant.[6]

> Should it be that you talk with this god and he hears you out/ [Pray for us] left behind on this miserable earth/ With the sky above us, grim and empty./ Plead with him that he may make sense and meaning of our lives.[7]

> Agnes, you who have suffered so unimaginably and so long, *you must be worthy to plead our cause.*[8]

Must Agnes die? Has the pastor grappled with the offense of death itself? This question insistently haunts the three remaining women. Has Agnes ("the lamb") been sacrificed to redeem their personal sins?

Those sins are exposed in the sequences that follow. Karin refuses to touch the corpse; Maria pretends to be loving, but screams and runs when love would require that she actually touch and kiss the dead body. But Anna loves in death as she had loved in life: Physically—and without hesitation—she cradles the body in her arms.

Agnes's death continues to push truths to the surface. Karin becomes more and more frantic to be released from the "tissue of lies" that imprisons her, represented variously in the film as her marriage, her social class, and her wealth. This is revealed most undeniably in the scene where Anna undresses her for the night, stripping off layer after layer of the formal clothes that hide Karin's body from the outside world. The memory of her mother touching her face in a rare moment of tenderness had been a *kairos* moment for Agnes.[9] Such grace is bountifully expanded in the miraculous scene where Karin and Maria meet, touch, and speak. For a few minutes, with their laughing faces set against a background red as the womb, the sisters wash away the bitterness of lives wasted in loveless marriages and futile jealousies. Here is a chance for rebirth, born of Agnes's birthlike death agony. This scene is acted out without words. It needs none. Our imaginations supply them.

But the sisters' reconciliation, not won through self-knowledge and spiritual recognition but in emotional crisis, collapses when they reenter their old lives. We're stranded inside the story, with no hope.

Or are we? Perhaps the movie does not aim to resolve conflicts or heal broken selves within the story world of the film itself, but to stimulate the viewer, who has the benefit of entering the consciousness of each of the four central characters. That is, we die with Agnes; we doubt with her pastor; and we return to life to challenge Maria's and Karin's inauthentic love. We suffer Agnes's excruciating (cross-bearing) physical pain and her struggle to interpret her suffering within a benevolent worldview.

At the end of the film, Anna remains alone in the house with Agnes's truth-telling diary. As Anna reads from it, we hear Agnes's voice:

> I closed my eyes and felt the breeze and the sun on my face. All my aches and pains were gone. The people I'm most fond of in the world were with me. I could hear them chatting round about me, I felt the presence of their bodies, the warmth of their hands. I closed my eyes tightly, trying to cling to the moment and thinking: Come what may, this is happiness. I can't wish for anything better. Now, for a few minutes, I can experience perfection. I feel a great gratitude to my life, which gives me so much.[10]

What does the ending mean? Charles B. Ketcham has written:

> It is clear that Agnes has triumphed over the terrors of the monstrous forces that beset her and has lived an authentic life in the tenuous and temporary manner in which that can only happen—brief moments of perfection, happiness and grace, in which the memory of pain persists but is superseded. . . . Life is now seen as . . . [having] the possibility but not the guarantee of integration, fulfillment, and authenticity.[11]

This is one possible interpretation.

There is one more path to authenticity that this film offers us: grace given through a person's life. Agnes's death does not mark the end of the movie, far from it. The film's structure resembles that of the sermon at her bedside. The first half is ritual and performance, while the second half strips away artifice to reveal a plea for mercy and understanding. Truth is a person, not an external revelation. "If it be so," then Agnes's great faith may be reborn within Anna, reader of the diary; within future readers of the diary; and within all of us who live, suffer, and die with Agnes through the experience of viewing the movie *Cries and Whispers*.

QUESTIONS 1. What does the title of the film—*Cries and Whispers*—mean? Where do "cries and whispers" appear in the movie, and what purpose do they serve as the story unfolds?

2. Flashbacks and dreams are important in this movie. Agnes recalls a Christmas celebration when she was a child, when she saw her mother and Maria watching *Twelfth Night*. What does this scene mean to Agnes? What kind of relationship does she appear to have with her mother? How might her relationship with her mother be connected to her life of faith?

3. After Agnes dies, her corpse appears to call out to each of her sisters, and then to Anna. How does each respond? Is this a dream, or in the movie's story world, does this really happen? What does this sequence mean?

4. Do you agree that this is a deeply religious movie? If so, is its tone predominantly hopeful or despairing? Discuss the film in the context of Paul's words to the Corinthians (1 Corinthians 13:12): "For now we see in a mirror, dimly, but then we will see face to face."

Secrets & Lies
Mike Leigh, Great Britain, 136 min.; Not Rated

Mike Leigh is the working-class person's director, attentive in his films to all the nuances of language and body movement that distinguish blue-collar workers in England from that island's omnipresent and overbearing upper crust. Yet *Secrets & Lies* is not limited to class or region. It confronts classism, racism, and even sexism—the three plagues that won't go away—yet it is neither preachy nor sentimental. At its heart it steadfastly maintains faith in the virtues that shone through *Cries and Whispers* as rarely fulfilled: honesty, love, and truthtelling. *Secrets & Lies* is a film that explodes pretense and gropes for authenticity.

PLOT Hortense, a young woman whose adoptive mother has recently died, decides to search for her birth mother. St. Catherine's House, repository of many secrets, provides her with the longed-for address of the mysterious woman who had given her up at birth twenty-six years earlier. When Hortense phones Cynthia, her birth mother, the older woman reacts with horror at the resurfacing of her child. The women meet in eleven minutes of the weirdest recognition scene since Shakespeare: Hortense is black; her mother is white.

Cynthia has been hiding this baby's birth from her other daughter, Roxanne, a tough brat who defies her, and from tidy sister-in-law Monica, her brother Maurice's wife. She has also buried this baby's birth from herself in self-pity over a life blasted by bad chances. Hortense's existence is not the only secret hiding in the family cupboards. Monica and Maurice are childless and grieving. Roxanne and Paul hide their love from the world.

Everyone gathers at Maurice's house for an elegant twenty-first birthday dinner for Roxanne. All the secrets come out. Everyone cries. The sisters have a chat. The sun shines down on Cynthia's tiny back garden.

REFLECTIONS This story could have been made into a syrupy melodrama. The emotions are big and bold; the secrets (illegitimacy! miscegenation!) are the very ones that Westerners most shudder at the thought of revealing. Moreover, the film is full of oppositions: two daughters, one black, one white. Educated daughter, poorly educated mother. Elegant home (Monica's), slummy home (Cynthia's).

Fancy bathrooms (Monica's and Hortense's), an outdoor loo (Cynthia's). Cynthia is unmistakably lower class: Her accent betrays her. Hortense, reared in a middle-class black family and university-trained, speaks comfortably in girl-talk with her girlfriend, but in the carefully modulated accents of the educated class everywhere else.

However, the narrative never slips into sentimentality. It moves gracefully from one person's story to the other, pulling out bits of the secrets until all are ready to be exposed. At no point does director Leigh raise an issue and then drop it; his intelligent script and restrained filmwork probe ever deeper until Maurice shouts, "I can't take it anymore!"

The drive in the film is not to claim its characters for religious belief and practice, but rather to lead them to discover where in life that harmony might be found. Photography provides an organizing idea for the film. Maurice is a professional photographer; a simple shot of his niece anchors us both in time (she was seven when this, one of the first of his works, was done; thus he's been in business about fourteen years) and mood (she's smiling in the shot but hasn't smiled much since, nor has he seen her recently). More centrally, photography records surfaces, image, façades; sorrow may lie beneath the image. Moreover, the professional's style may reveal the secrets of his own heart.[12]

Moviemaking is both like and unlike photography—it records images on film stock, which are then made available to be viewed. The way the images are arranged shapes the way we understand what they mean or how we respond to them. Mike Leigh understands this. He does not use the flashbacks, dreams, and voice-over that Bergman used in *Cries*. He does not want to transport us to a dream world, but to keep us squarely in this one. His movie style (very direct and earthy) is appropriate to its subject matter: the lives of ordinary people in modern-day London, who, like us, are struggling to make a living, get along with sons and daughters, find a bit of romance, and somehow live with their guilt and shame over past mistakes. Leigh wants to make their sorrows ours, so that we can be part of the journey toward authenticity, healing, and celebration that the film shows us.

Of all the wonderfully photographed sequences in the movie, three shine with an economy of images and a richness of feeling. The first is the graveside service that opens the film. The second is Hortense's first encounters with her mother, Cynthia. The third, divided into two pairs and an epilogue, seals the movie's right to be called a modern classic.

The opening sequence reveals the movie's tone, intent, and rhythm. We see ornate tombstones tumbling together in an overgrown cemetery. The camera cuts to the mourners, seen from the low-angle perspective of the gravediggers, whose bodies and faces almost fill the screen. We feel as though we are either *in* the grave or *digging the grave* with these men. Taking its time as the mourners sing three verses of "How Great Thou Art," the camera allows us to see faces: all professions, from workers to the elegant. Who has died? A high crane shot reveals a floral wreath that spells "Mum," with mourners arranged in perfect symmetry around her grave.

The music and words of the hymn unify the cuts: "When Christ shall come with shout of acclamation . . . what joy shall fill my heart." As the roving camera settles on the face of a young woman, we see that at least one person is not comforted by the words of harmony and peace. We witness and enter into her silent grief as a haunting cello melody swells up over the steady music of the hymn. The song speaks of the authentic self grounded in a sure knowledge of God's love. Hortense, we will learn, lacks this assurance; she is motherless, without a sure and solid identity.

The cello melody signals a longing for a life that is whole, honest, and loving. At the heart of human life is a great emptiness, a longing to have someone cherish you just as you are—to call you by name, to worry about you when you're late coming home, and to miss you if you're not there. The child's face lights up when her mother comes into the room. This radiance provides a sure resting place for the self, even during those years when the desire for freedom trumps the memory of affection.

Hortense longs for this closeness—with her birth mother. She asks the basic questions about authenticity: Why was I born? Who is the woman who chose to throw me away? She elects to take the quest into her own hands. As Tom Hanks and Meg Ryan moved closer geographically in *Sleepless in Seattle*, Hortense begins to close in on her mother, Cynthia, across London. In the best mystery-detective style, the shots that show the detective on the trail alternate with shots of the quarry (*cross-cutting*).[13] Cynthia is an unlikely object of desire: slovenly, tired, whining, careless about herself and her housekeeping. Furthermore, she already has a daughter: a daughter who resents her prying mother; a daughter with secrets of her own.

How does authenticity work into the film's overall movement toward reconciliation? The encounter between mother and daughter is played in various emotional scales that range from horror to comedy. Yet the importance of this meeting to each of them is underscored.

When Hortense first phones, Cynthia is at her lowest point. Roxanne, furious at her mother's invasion of her private life and space, has just thrown her mother down and stalked out. When Cynthia hears Hortense announce that she is her discarded child, she can barely take in the information. Shocked, she hangs up the phone and runs to the sink to vomit.

The phone rings again. The framing of this sequence of shots portrays Cynthia's fear and revulsion at the resurrection of a vile episode from her past, and it also sucks us into her life. She hears the phone, turns, wipes her hands and her mouth, and moves in horror toward the hated object. Just as her face comes close to the camera, the camera cuts to the phone ringing alone in the dark hall. Cynthia's large back invades the space. We no longer see her face as she speaks, but we are conscious of her shabby and ill-fitting clothes and the cramped space in the hall.

The camera now crosscuts between Cynthia and Hortense as the younger woman pleads to meet with her. This part would be easy to play for sentiment, with mother and daughter joyfully and tearfully reunited. Instead, each woman is kept suspended in *dead time* as Cynthia absorbs the message this voice delivers and Hortense waits, fearful that this slender thread of connection with her own identity will be lost.[14]

After she has jotted down Hortense's number, Cynthia sits on the stairs to think. Her physical position on the stairs duplicates that of one earlier in the film, when Monica had pondered (as if for the first time) her rejection of the fatherless Roxanne and her scorn for her sister-in-law, Cynthia.[15]

Cynthia phones Hortense for a meeting. The discovery scene has four parts: the first phone calls, already described; the meeting in front of the Holborn tube station in London; the women's conversation in a café near the station; and a long ride from Holborn back to Cynthia's house. Eleven minutes of the movie are devoted to the face-to-face encounter, in which Cynthia's constant refrain is first, "This must be a great disappointment for you," when she thinks Hortense has the wrong woman, and then, "I must be a great disappointment to you," when she realizes she is indeed Hortense's mother.

The gap in the women's educations and life aspirations is painfully apparent, emphasized because mother and daughter are seen sitting side by side, facing the camera in flat, documentary style. The framing is deliberate: The medium shots show their faces clearly but also show position and body movement.[16] Before long, however, expectation turns life around for both women. Their next encounters are shown in elegant locations, facing each other as equals as they open their hearts.

The final sequences in the film, a dinner and a reunion, blend authenticity with home and celebration. The setting is the meal—the birthday party toward which all the strands of the movie's story have been leading. This final section of the film is divided into several parts: the entry of the guests (Hortense is almost turned away), the obligatory displaying of the fine house, the appetizers, and the dinner. This ritual celebration is somewhat like the first half of the pastor's graveside sermon in *Cries and Whispers*. It has all the right moves and all the right words. There is tension in the air, but generally everyone is on their best behavior.

The elaborate word-dance at the table is tough, but it's played like comedy: We the viewers can laugh because we have more knowledge than the diners do. (We know that Hortense does not work at the box factory, for instance; we know that Hortense is not used to lying about her work.)

Now comes the move toward truth, and it comes at a ritualistic moment—when the birthday girl blows out her candles and makes a wish. There is something about communion (the meal) that stimulates truth-telling. Cynthia, overwhelmed by the intimacy of the celebration, reveals that Hortense is her *other* daughter. How is this announcement treated? No long shots of the appetizer table as we had earlier—no medium shots of diners enjoying a garden barbecue—but close-ups of faces, one after the other, revealing first mystification, then horror, then embarrassment. There's no escape from the truth. There are no words to sugar over such an unexpected revelation.

Authenticity: What is it? "Tell them who you are, sweetheart," Cynthia cries to the startled Hortense, who reenters the room just after Cynthia has blurted out her secret. This is what Hortense has been trying to discover during the entire film: not the name she was born with, but where she can find her spiritual and emotional home. She cannot respond. She will not be able to understand who *she* is until she is embraced by a household that understands who *they* are, who tell the truth and "share our pain."

This understanding comes, oddly enough, not simply through Maurice's confessions or Cynthia's, but through the backstage work of social rejects Paul and Jane. Jane, Maurice's assistant and a guest at the party, is a silent sufferer whose past of child abuse is only hinted at. Paul is Roxanne's sweetheart, who cherishes her and lights her life. When he speaks the loving words that encourage Roxanne to return home to "listen" to her mother's story, and when Jane tells Maurice that he is an ideal father to his household (even though he is childless), the poison of decades of secrets and lies evaporates, and healing can begin.

Like the "fools" in *Forrest Gump* and *Sling Blade* (see chapter 6), Paul and Jane give voice to charity and forgiveness. In response, the authentic self cannot be found until we enter another person's life and share his or her anguish—Maurice pleads for truth, Hortense comforts Cynthia despite her own grief, Paul reaches out to Roxanne, and the family includes Jane in its circle of belonging.

The final sequence in the film—an epilogue to the celebration—takes place in Cynthia's back garden. It had been the scene of an earlier, nasty confrontation between Cynthia and Roxanne. Now the focus is on the rundown greenhouse (we see Roxanne's old highchair inside), where two young faces looking in are framed by two separate pieces of glass. Side by side, Hortense and Roxanne gingerly explore the subject of their coming life together: "Do you feel like we're sisters?" "Yeah." Neither has to put on a false face, either a dignified or a sullen one; both wear the beautiful smiles of happy children. Each speaks freely and happily. They agree that "it's simpler" to tell the truth to people who ask who they are.

The film closes quietly with a crane shot from high above the garden, which reminds us of the crane shot of the funeral service in the beginning of the film. That earlier shot had displayed a community unified in grief for a dead mother; this one reveals two women, one black, one white, with a live "Mum" in the center. They are all sunning themselves in Cynthia's transformed "kingdom" space. Cynthia sighs: "This is the life, ain't it?"

QUESTIONS 1. How does color (black daughter, white mother) affect the film as a whole? If the daughter had been white, how would the film have been different? (How big an issue is race in this film?)

2. The movie dwells on its characters' sexuality: Cynthia; Roxanne; Monica and Maurice; Hortense. What are some of the ways the film grapples with issues of sexual morality and birth ethics? For instance, Roxanne calls her mother a "slag" (slut). Does the movie support this criticism? Why might Roxanne react in this way? Cynthia is concerned that each of her daughters protect herself against unwanted pregnancy. Does this reflect her desire that she personally had never given birth to these young women?

3. In many movies, one person represents a moral center for the film as a whole. Who fulfills that role in this film? If you think the role is divided among many characters, who are they, and how do they act?

4. Why do you think Mike Leigh has inserted so many photography sessions into the movie? In what ways does this unusual technique support or detract from the main concerns in the film?

5. Movies are frequently criticized or praised based on their representation of the "real" world. Is this a "realistic" movie in the sense that its people and situations resemble life as you know it? Do you find its story line believable and convincing? In real life, do you think reconciliations such as the ones shown in this film are possible?

Alienation presents the quest for authenticity not through domestic drama but through movies that push the idea of separation to extremes. Here, alienation is separation from self, society, God, and this present life. To understand and overcome this feeling of powerlessness may mean a trip to the far country—outer space—or into the future. Within these fantasies, it is the nature of human existence itself that is explored—human life with its power to create, covenant, or destroy.

SCENE:
TAKE: **3**

ALIENATION

Star Trek
Solaris
Blade Runner
Contact

INTRODUCTION

> *"I've done questionable things. . . . Nothing the god of Biomechanics wouldn't let you in heaven for."*
>
> *Replicant Roy Batty to Eldon Tyrell, his maker, in* Blade Runner

The writer of a recent newspaper article laments the "shallow nihilism of modern movies," which have arisen, this obviously cineplexed-out author writes, from "the same morbid, chaotic, angst-ridden, post–World War I, dark, creative murk that fostered the bitter cynical work" of many German dramatists, artists, and movie directors in the 1920s.[1] Traditionally, the summer movie season can be a tough time for those of us who like small, reflective films, or at least movies with a solid story and intriguing style — *African Queen*, for instance, or *Rear Window*, or *Secrets & Lies*.

The newspaper writer criticized specifically director Luc Besson's then-current film, *The Fifth Element* (starring Bruce Willis), but he also included *Face/Off* and *Sling Blade*. All three are heavily borrowed, he believes, from the movies of Fritz Lang, particularly his spooky classic *M* (1931) and the groundbreaking *Metropolis* (1926), in which a ruthless businessman commissions a mad scientist to construct a cyborg to replace his underground workers, who are inconveniently prone to sickness, accidents, and death. Why does this writer object to today's movies? It's not that the newer films are not original, but that many of them "frequently have no logic. They have little humanity or there's no moral to the story. All the interest and reason in the story disappear. Sometimes the narrative drive disappears." In other words, there's no story, no context, no point. Why make the movie at all?

The problem with this analysis is that his basic point is right — many recent movies have no point — but his examples are flawed. *Face/Off*, for instance, has both sappy moments and heavy violence, but nonetheless it poses difficult questions about human identity: Who are we? What do we want, and what drives us to pursue these goals? How do we judge whether what we desire is ethical? What is the role of the church in shaping personal and social behaviors? Rather than presenting an easy opposition between the good guys and the bad guys, which is the usual tactic of summer blockbusters and a mainstay of American storytelling, *Face/Off* blurs the lines between good and evil and allows both heroes room for moral growth.[2]

Sling Blade and *Blade Runner* are also mentioned as heirs of moviemaking that sprang up in a time of "moral degeneracy."

If movies reflect the times we live in, the writer asks, why pro-
duce such dark pieces as *The Fifth Element* [he could have
included *Batman and Robin, Air Force One,* and *Con Air* in his
assessment] at a time we have "no war, no threat, global stability, falling crime, a booming stock market, low unemployment, minimal inflation, high church attendance" and other
rosy pluses to celebrate?[3] He could even have added that, not
content with the disappearance of the usual villains—Soviet
spies and various miscreants—(and bored with the clichéd
Nazi punks), the director of *Air Force One* created a new set of
villains, ultranationalists from the Russian republic of Kazak-
stan (who in the movie resemble New Yorkers more than they
resemble their real-life models, the Asian Kazaks).[4]

REFLECTIONS The article makes an odd connection between
subject matter (dark plots, creepy villains, fire-
ball special effects) and *quality* that I find suspect: Cheery is
good, pessimistic is bad. Movies that tackle the subject of
alienation—personal, social, religious—come off badly. But
alienation (in religious language, *sin*) drives most narratives.
Surely we don't want to limit our movie plots to sugar-candied
and sentimental moments.

Biblical narratives don't shy away from alienation. "Screen
moments"—scenes in movies where the hero or heroine is
rewarded for a life of virtue (as the camera moves in for a
close-up and violin music trembles shamelessly)—are few in
number in the Bible and are generally preceded by gross
infraction or personal suffering. The Bible frankly presents
the tough lot of most people: Ruth married Boaz, but only
after years of backbreaking labor in the fields and a life as an
outsider; Abraham was rewarded by God, but only after being
tested on the mountaintop; Tamara was vindicated, but she
first was cast out of doors by an unjust father-in-law; Joseph
was elevated to national leadership, but only after near-death
in the bottom of a well and imprisonment in Egypt. Many of

the psalms express laments of those who have suffered injustice or strain under guilt, physical misery, and social isolation.[5]

The Bible's stories, however, are presented within the embrace of divine covenant. Covenant allows the alienated one or ones to return to the arms of the waiting father or mother, in the language of Jesus' parable of the prodigal son. The anguish of the sufferer is soothed by trust in a loving God.

> In the LORD I take refuge. . . .
> The LORD is in his holy temple;
> the LORD's throne is in heaven.
> (Psalm 11:1*a*, 4*a*)

Although the sufferer may hope that the wicked will be punished, perhaps the strongest need is to be heard, to have an advocate:

> Your faithfulness is as firm as the heavens.
> (Psalm 89:2*b*)

Perhaps what the writer of the article I've quoted regrets is not the *presence* of violence and noisy special effects, but the *absence* of a system of values that all of us could endorse. The edginess in many modern films may not reflect worry about immediate problems such as war or unemployment. They may reflect rather that directors and producers are not sure what audiences consider disgusting and what they consider desirable. Do we have a shared vision of what the world should be? Do directors, producers, and audiences all find violence against persons and groups basically disgusting, no matter how often we see violent acts on the screen? Do we want to find a more just way to live together?[6] It isn't the presence of sorrow or injustice in a film that makes us uneasy—Andrei Tarkovsky commented that the artist who expresses his time must touch all its "running sores"—instead, it's the failure to identify the suffering and injustice as somehow wrong, an offense to our common moral sensibility. Representations of extreme violence can function like the prophetic oracles of Jeremiah and Hosea to heighten our awareness of social or personal wrongdoing. But the underlying vision of wholeness must be secure for such prophesies to be effective; otherwise, we become confused and disoriented.

Two examples of such disorientation occur in the popular movie *Air Force One*. The sterling Harrison Ford (much given in recent years to playing characters of great integrity, courage, and loyalty, as in *The Fugitive* and *Witness*), portrays a United States President, an Armed Services veteran, who thinks clearly and courageously and intends to stand on his word. In a speech (delivered partly in Russian), he promises that America will in the future move swiftly and boldly to protect suffering groups around the world (an allusion, perhaps, to the failure of the West to act soon enough to head off ethnic cleansing in Bosnia or Rwanda). He says, "Real peace is not just absence of conflict. It is the presence of justice"—a variation on the slogan "no peace without justice" that animates social justice movements in this country.

The movie tiptoes around issues such as the U.S. military's role in Iraq, where our bombs are said to have killed 100,000 or more defenseless soldiers at the end of the Persian Gulf War. The effectiveness of this bit of information is removed, however, because it is placed in the mouth of the villain. Similarly, the movie plays with but does not fully explore the political position of refusing to negotiate with terrorists and weighing a few lives against many. Most disturbingly, it shows the President killing one of his attackers—not offscreen, but in full view, complete with the sound of a neck snapping. There is also a scene where a most sympathetic character, the President's press secretary, is murdered at close range. Two rules in traditional storytelling have been violated: Never show the hero—in this case, the leader of the Free World—committing a violent act; and never assault and kill a defenseless person with whom the audience has become identified.

These "rules" arise from assumptions about human behavior that cross centuries and cultures: that the innocent or vulnerable should be protected; the strong should be active to protect them; children should not be harmed; unarmed or disabled persons (even villains) should not be killed in cold blood; and society, not the individual, has the responsibility for serving justice.

Filmmakers ignore these assumptions at their peril. Alfred Hitchcock once included a little boy in a movie as the carrier of a dangerous bomb. The bomb exploded, "killing" not only expendable extras (the people on the bus the boy was riding on) but also the child himself. Such tragedies happen in real life. Perhaps because many of our popular stories are built on the hope that the world in all its parts works toward the good, we find the representation of the deaths of children unacceptable. Even vigilante justice must be carefully managed in narrative; we may applaud the execution of the bad guys, but there must be justification and a fair fight. Justice and mercy may be at odds temporarily, but rarely is one present without the other in our public storymaking.[7]

The movies discussed in this chapter confront alienation—personal, social, and spiritual—through science fiction, a story medium that often reflects a desire to find shared moral values and to search for ultimate meaning. If a film like _Contact_ slightly misses the mark or the _Star Trek_ films and television episodes sometimes become repetitive, they are to be praised as much for what they don't accomplish as for what they do. They at least know the issues (e.g., the longing for home, the poison of human greed, the desire for knowledge, and the unacceptability of poverty and war) and attempt to deal with them inventively and responsibly. They consciously arouse the audience's sympathy and fear in order to make room for purification of heart—time-honored methods practiced by both Greek dramatists and American preachers.

Alienation is defined by its opposites, belonging and wholeness. Alienation in this century exploded with the Holocaust in Western Europe and the genocides in Armenia; the fire storms of Hiroshima, Nagasaki, and Dresden; and an increasing number of ecological disasters. We have new anxieties to exhibit and new ways to display them. Just as the gargoyles on medieval cathedrals put human deformity and transgression on public display, movies have matched those visions of the world with an astonishing parade of human oddities and alienation. We may be dismayed at much of what we see at the cineplex. But whenever a movie's director and producers have a strong vision of what a truly whole and healthy life can be, the results can stimulate us to reflect and to change.

GOING TO THE MOVIES

Star Trek
Gene Roddenberry; original television series 1966, three additional series and nine films to date

Events have a way of blurring the boundaries between the real and the imaginary. Take the summer of 1997, for instance. If *Men in Black* harkened back to the good old days of *Ghostbusters* in its playful battle with slimy alien creatures, a movie like *Contact* meshed eerily with the daily bulletins and NASA photos from Mars and the troubled space station Mir.[8] Ellie Arroway (Jodie Foster), the earnest astronomer in *Contact*, is intent on intercepting signals from outer space that prove the existence of other life-forms in the universe. She reminds us of one of the purposes of the numerous space missions: to establish some perspective on our earthly life. Robert Zemeckis, director of *Contact,* has said, "It's not about aliens; it's about us. . . . The reason to go to the moon is what? To look back at the earth."[9]

From its beginnings on television in 1966, Gene Roddenberry's *Star Trek* series has suffered the indignities of lukewarm ratings and unbelieving studios over its thirty-plus years and various incarnations, but its fans worldwide continue to praise the daring and invention of its concepts and the occasional brilliance of its episodes. Who among Trekkers could forget the satisfactions of the original series' "Space Seed" (episode 24), "The City on the Edge of For-ever" (episode 28), "Patterns of Force" (episode 52); or *Star Trek: The Next Generation's* "The Perfect Mate" (episode 121) or "The Best of Both Worlds" (parts I and II, episodes 74 and 75) or "Yesterday's Enterprise" (episode 63)?

What the television studio executives may not have realized when they allowed *Star Trek* to surface was that this program—and its eight (soon-to-be nine) spin-off films—is much more than otherworldly entertainment, a thrilling ride into hyperspace. As phenomenon or as individual episodes, it promotes virtues that are as startling to today's world as those Jesus preached to his: tolerance, love, peace on earth, and active work to defeat disease and poverty. Furthermore, in *Star Trek,* classical music and serious books—from Berlioz to Shakespeare to Herman Melville—can be found just about everywhere. And criticism that the possession and expansion of scientific knowledge will ultimately lead to "mass destruction" is regarded as particularly primitive and shortsighted.

Echoing the messages of Andrei Tarkovsky's *Solaris* and the more recent *Contact,* the crew of the *Enterprise* praises space exploration as the step that unites humanity and diverts Earth's attention away from self-destructive war. It shows human beings that they are "not alone in the universe." In *Star Trek: First Contact* (1996), for instance, the images of an ideal human civilization are insistently presented: a close shot of a black hand in a white one; women and men working side by side on equal tasks; humans and nonhumans dedicated to keeping the peace in the galaxy. The "unknown" is not imagined as terrifying, but as benign, even loving. The first words of the first extraterrestrial beings, when they step onto planet Earth, are: "Live long and prosper."

PLOT In a 1967 television episode, Captain James Kirk of the starship *Enterprise* deposited a genetically engineered superman named Khan and his crew on a distant planet, well stocked with food and supplies. Now, fifteen years later, the outcasts have become prey to hunger, dislocation, and vicious space beasts, and Khan wants revenge on the promoted Admiral Kirk, no longer in direct command of the *Enterprise*. Kahn lures two *Enterprise* crew members to his lair; hijacks the Genesis project, a research program designed to create new life in lifeless territory; and attacks the *Enterprise*. Kirk's dearest friend and former first officer, Spock, is killed when he saves the *Enterprise* crew from certain death.

REFLECTIONS *Star Wars* gives a good ride. I saw the original films in the theater in the 1970s and cheered their reissue in 1997. However, despite its exemplary "good" characters Obi-Wan (Ben) Kenobi and Luke Skywalker (along with their irrepressible androids), and even despite the rebel flair of Han Solo, *Star Wars* is religion lite—a comic book battle between Good and Evil, with The Force waiting in the wings to enable the good folks to pull themselves out of the pit at the last minute. If one role of movies is to help us figure out how to live, then I'd place *Stars War* along with *The Karate Kid* (which I *also* like!)—as "great entertainment constructed . . . out of bits of American pop culture," a fantasy that "give[s] voice to our deepest longings and speaks to our hope for the future of society of ourselves,"[10] but not very satisfying *religiously*.

What if great entertainment, stirring special effects, and good message were to be combined with complex story-telling, compelling characterization, and commitment to examine personal and social morality? What if thoughtful examination of religious belief were thrown in? This formula wouldn't sell, right? But it did, and it has—on television since 1966 (reruns 1970–1986), and in movie theaters since 1979. It's *Star Trek*.

An attempt to capture a similar combination of cutting-edge technology, morality, and religion has appeared in recent years with *Dune* and *Stargate*, but nothing quite equals the seriousness of *Star Trek*'s daring mission: to explore what society might look and feel like if all ages, ethnicities, genders, and degrees of "humanness" lived and worked together. *Star Trek II: The Wrath of Khan* represents *Star Trek*'s overall innovative and relentless exploration of moral problems and insistence on human goodness. Its optimistic vision is the affirmation that sustained the best of the ancient tragedies and animates a community of faith secure in the promises of a faithful and loving God.

As one Trekker recently reminded me, *Star Trek* isn't really science fiction so much as it is utopian, exploring ideal human behavior.[11] Money is not an issue; wealth is no longer a driving force. Different ethnicities and different species work together and get along. On board the *Enterprise* over the years have been, among other "aliens," the indomitable Spock, who, as the doctor (Leonard "Bones" McCoy) repeatedly reminds him, is "not human" (he is half-Vulcan), and the appealing Data (who serves decades later on another *Enterprise*), an android in constant search of his own humanity. This is a crew dedicated to keeping the peace and to exploring, rather than conquering space or defeating aliens.

Khan appears at first to follow a standard revenge plot:

Khan feels he has been wronged and will stop at nothing to get even with Kirk. Khan's beloved wife has been killed. Khan's son pleads for his father to be content with having gained a ship and supplies, and then with possessing the Genesis technology. The biblical message is clear: "Vengeance is mine, I will repay," says the Lord (Romans 12:19 NRSV). This motif is repeated more directly in *Star Trek: First Contact*, where the *Enterprise*'s Captain Picard is nearly derailed by his desire to "get even" with the Borg, a war-minded, machine-like alien race who earlier (in *The Next Generation*'s "The Best of Both Worlds") had kidnapped and tried to assimilate him into their collective. Picard is called back to himself when he remembers Captain Ahab's thundering speech of rage in *Moby Dick*.

Opposing the revenge plot in *Khan* is the equally compelling plot of the quest for the meaning of life. Kirk is aging; what would make him young again? Is it love? Is it to resume command of his old ship? Is it some scientific fix? Oddly enough, when Kirk says, "I feel young again," it is after his dearest friend Spock has sacrificed himself and has been launched out into space, apparently to rest on a lifeless planet that is being reborn through the Genesis explosion that Spock diverted away from the starship.

At the end of the film, Kirk is reading a very large book. It may be Charles Dickens's *A Tale of Two Cities*, Spock's birthday gift to Kirk, from which we hear both the opening words ("It was the best of times; it was the worst of times") and the closing ones, having to do with a friend's self-sacrifice to save his look-alike ("It is a far, far better thing I do than I have ever done before"). But it could also be the Bible, Dickens's inspiration for this and all his novels. Khan's personal reading was *Moby Dick* and *King Lear*, from which he had extracted words of rage at the injustice of the universe. Kirk's is Dickens or the Scriptures.[12]

QUESTIONS 1. The crew of the *Enterprise* works with a federation of more than one hundred planets to keep the peace in the galaxy. Among the enemies of peace are a strange collective race called the Borg, whose stated aim is to conquer and assimilate "flawed humans," to "become perfect." How does this reflect our current obsessions with biomedical technology such as prenatal diagnosis, gene therapy, and cloning?

2. In the film *Star Trek: First Contact,* members of the *Enterprise* crew have come to Earth in the year 2063 to help launch the world's first vehicle that can travel at warp speed. One crew member remarks that he finds it ironic that an "instrument of mass destruction" (a nuclear missile) has been converted to inaugurate an era of peace. Do you think it possible that the nations of the world might ever invest as much in health care and food for the hungry as we do in weapons systems? Is this a reasonable or desirable wish? Why or why not?

3. Questions about ethics arise in each episode: What about genetic engineering and cloning? What is the morality of seeking to create life? How do you meet death?

Solaris
Andrei Tarkovsky, Russia, 1972, 167 min.; Not Rated

Only in recent years has Andrei Tarkovsky's work become known in America. Partly due to his career-long struggle with the Soviet film and political bureaucracies (which severely censored his work) and partly due to distribution problems, his movies were seen in the United States only in badly cut or dubbed versions. Even though Tarkovsky was able to complete only eight films in his lifetime, his work has put him in the ranks of the world's greatest directors, a filmmaker whose intense spiritual and artistic visions are beautifully meshed. No one who wants to examine the theme of alienation from a religious perspective could fail to consider his work.[13]

I had planned at first to examine *Stalker* (Tarkovsky, 1979); its acting and the beauty of its visual images are overwhelming. One recent winter, when I was in Strasbourg, France, the local movie theater played *Solaris* on a Thursday night, a school night for lycée students. To my surprise, I found myself in the same long and pushy line of twelve-to-sixteen-year-old boys who are my usual showtime movie companions for the U.S. blockbusters. Nervously, I made my way to the balcony, where I could see that the theater (a 200-seater) was completely packed. The noise level showed no signs of lowering even when the lights went down.

Solaris began slowly, deliberately drawing the character of psychologist Kris Kelvin against the backdrop of tense family relations and the specter of his father's unhappy friend, an astronaut whose disturbing messages about his findings in outer space were ignored by the space industry. I looked around. Those gum-cracking, fidgety boys had stopped roaming around the theater and had quietly taken their seats. For the remaining two hours of the movie, no one in the theater moved or spoke, except occasionally to gasp or cry out as the story wound tighter and tighter. At film's end, the theater broke into applause. (*Solaris* may be little-known in America, but in Europe, it and *Stalker* have cult status.)

This had been my own response the first time I saw *Solaris*, despite the film's murky picture quality due to faulty film stock provided by Soviet suppliers. For Tarkovsky, the energy and rhythm of a film is in the imagery, not in the speed of editing. Unlike many American "disaster" movies (*Die Hard, Twister*), which cut every few seconds to move the pace along at breakneck speed, sometimes Tarkovsky does not cut for as long as ten minutes. So much is happening in the frame before you that you are spellbound. For movies such as *Stalker* and *Solaris* that are so rich in religious and spiritual imagery, this more measured pace allows the viewer to simultaneously experience the excitement of impending danger and reflect on the theological and ethical implications of the story.

PLOT A number of expeditions have been sent to the planet Solaris, one manned by the astronaut Burton, whose disturbing findings were discredited when he returned. Kris Kelvin is dispatched to the failing space station to investigate mysterious reports of alien sightings and disappearing astronauts. Kris is a cold fish. His contempt for and coldness toward his wife led to her suicide. He has a troubled relationship with his father, a warm and intelligent man who prizes his son's intelligence but regrets his hostility toward love and affection. "Men like you should not go into space," his father warns the detached and emotionless Kris.

Once on the space station, Kris encounters dead and not-so-dead beings in the forms of a videotaped suicide speech by his friend, the astronaut Gibarian; the embodied images of the other scientists' fantasies; and his own guilt-ridden memories of his dead wife and mother. Kris is completely transformed by what he learns about himself through this space journey and returns to Earth (perhaps) to reconcile with his father.

REFLECTIONS *Solaris* follows the journey plan common to so many great narratives: Travel through space and time parallels the discovery of the self's relationship with God and other persons. The film's originality lies in the way it has adapted a famous Polish science fiction novel as the vehicle for this journey of spiritual transformation—that is, it looks and feels like a science fiction movie, but it's more. It combines cutting-edge scientific and technical knowledge with all the markers of a culture alive to art, music, history, and religion, while giving careful attention to issues of guilt, responsibility, forgiveness, and redemption. What is wrong at the space station is not that slimy monsters have invaded or that the oxygen generators are not functioning. What is wrong is the failings of the human heart. The film explores the possibility that a person might atone for past actions.

Early on, the movie sets its dominant mode: What is to be prized is not the technology that set a space station in the sky light-years away, but rather the beauty of the river, the marshes, the lush green plants, and flowers that surround the father's *dacha* (country home). The beginning of Kris's transformation occurs in the hours before he leaves for Solaris, when he stands in the rain looking out onto the river that runs beside his father's house. This lovely sequence is done in four long takes that lovingly dwell on the plants beneath the water, the flowers that float on it, the trees beside it, the mist above it. The languid still shots contrast sharply with the rapid-paced, long, ugly journey his father's friend Burton takes from the country back into a city laced with the poisonous fumes of its endless freeways.

Kris's actual trip is compressed into one swift sequence. The real interest lies in who and what he will find at the space station. The station is a mess. Its few remaining inhabitants behave strangely; one even refuses to show himself, although Kris catches a glimpse of a strange creature whisking around a corner. The mood is one not so much of despair but of desperation. The proximity of the planet Solaris to Earth, it seems, has allowed the astronauts' dreams, fantasies, and guilty memories to materialize. One scientist is plagued by the apparition of a very young girl—a Dostoyevsky touch.[14]

Kris also becomes afflicted by memories, principally by dreams of his cold and beautiful mother and by the materializations of his dead wife, Hari, young and lovely as in life but branded with the unmistakable sign of her death: a needle mark on her arm. Not surprisingly, Kris tries to rid himself of this apparition, sending Hari off in a space capsule. She reappears, and the power of her essential *humanity* begins to captivate him. Kris is given an opportunity to relive the past to undo the harm caused by his own actions.[15] Unlike the other scientists, who dismiss their apparitions as unreal and pesky, Kris confronts his guilt and tries to compensate for his evil-doing.

Kris is forced to examine what it means to be human and whether values such as love, affirmation, hope, and taking responsibility for your actions have any power. Unlike the novel from which *Solaris* was adapted, which emphasizes the fragility of human values and the emptiness of human life (versus the power of technology), the movie drives its hero toward forgiveness (of himself) and reconciliation (with all those he has hurt). "Knowledge is valid only when it is based on morality."[16] Tarkovsky's understanding of the universe is devoutly God-centered, unlike that of the novelist, who believed that the best humans could do in the face of the unknown is simply to endure.

Two features of this movie strike me with great force every time I see it. One is that the hero increasingly identifies with the Earth and its regenerative powers over the sterility of space. The startling concluding scene of the film, when Kris kneels at his father's feet in front of the *dacha*, returns Kris "home" in all the ways we have explored in earlier chapters. Added to this are the meditations stimulated by the various artworks that float through the film: a copy of *Don Quixote;* a picture of Brueghel's *Hunters in the Snow*; a copy of Andrei Roublev's icon *The Trinity*; and snatches of Bach. Art is rich and timeless; it calls out memories of love and of the Divine, in contrast with memories of painful, barely suppressed loss and guilt. Art enriches our common life and connects us with each other. As Tarkovsky himself once wrote, the purpose of art is "to turn and loosen the human soul, making it receptive to good."[17]

QUESTIONS 1. *Solaris* is another movie with "bookends": the story is enclosed inside long, languid takes that invite the viewer to meditate on the meaning—not simply the events—inside the frame. How do you interpret the final sequence? Why is it raining inside the dacha? Is this happening on Solaris, or back on Earth? Has Kris ever left Earth?

2. Who are the "guests" on the spaceship? What is their function in the lives of the astronauts? What do they add to the movie's theological explorations?

3. Do you believe that a person can ever atone for past mistakes? If so, how?

Blade Runner
Ridley Scott, 1982, 119 min.; R

One night when my daughters Catherine and Sarah were watching *Solaris* with some friends, one boy called out, "Hey, I recognize this story: I just saw *Event Horizon*." He was right, of course; *Event Horizon* (1997) is, as one reviewer discreetly put it, "inspired" by Tarkovsky's great film. So is *Blade Runner;* so is *Gattaca* (1997). But whereas *Event Horizon* trades on horror (newspaper adds scream: "Frightening as *The Exorcist!*") and is not a good movie, *Blade Runner* is as intense as *Solaris* in its probing of the theological and ethical dimensions of science. It is furthermore a stunning work of film art—in short, a classic.

PLOT Rick Deckard (Harrison Ford), former Blade Runner (a member of the futuristic police force), has a killer new job: to track down six genetically engineered replicants, artificial humans, who have slipped into the Los Angeles of A.D. 2019. Their aim: either to wrest more life-years from their maker, Eldon Tyrell of Tyrell Corporation, or to avenge themselves on all who had a part in their cruel creation.

Several problems surface for Deckard during this *High Noon-*style showdown: He falls in love with Rachael (Sean Young), a young woman who is a replicant; he must survive in a society that appears to be infested with replicants and amoral humans; and he may be a replicant himself, one who is developing old-fashioned "human" emotions such as love and conscience.

REFLECTIONS *Blade Runner* presents a world like George Orwell's *1984,* a world where all of humanity's worst fears are realized: Human enterprise—through its greed and poor planning—has unleashed lifelike forms ("more human than human," their creator describes his newest model) that have turned against their creators. It is also a movie that belongs solidly to detective fiction and film noir. The hero, Deckard, was on the inside as a Blade Runner; he knows the ropes; he got out while he could—all the movie clichés we know from Humphrey Bogart's films.[18] In his mind and by his personal moral code, Deckard stands outside the sinister workings of a massively controlled, futuristic police state, where "commerce is our goal" and no thought is given to the ethical implications of technological advances. The very qualities that made him a renegade on the police force—his cynicism and his reflection—make him the ideal person to hunt and "retire" the escaped cyborgs.

As in *Unforgiven, Blade Runner* runs a standard story line—the hunt for villains by a man who stands outside the law—against a solid and unmistakably religious quest that questions every step of that plot. *Unforgiven* begins with a scrolled text.

Blade Runner does also, and it tells a hideous tale. Human invention, the glorious gift of reason that sets persons just below the angels (Psalm 8), has been perverted to create beings who are "superior in strength and agility, and at least equal in intelligence," to their engineers. Why on earth *do* this? Answer A is that these creatures can serve human needs, sort of like a pet rock. Answer B is that "replicants [a]re used Off-world as slave labor, in the hazardous exploration and colonization of other planets."

These are not just machines, however. Their creator admits — and Pris, one replicant, emphasizes — that they are "physical" — they are flesh and blood! Moreover, while they are not created with emotions, they can acquire them through memory implants, but, more critically, also through life experience. That is, they begin as machines but can become fully vested with human feeling — love, hate, longing, regret, fear of death.

So the replicants burst into view with a history of violence for which they will be punished, according to the "law" of Earth: They have killed twenty-three people and are themselves to be killed. They are considered trespassers on the earth that gave them birth. (It seems that their real crime, though, was to rebel against their enslavement, not to kill, for life is cheap in A.D. 2019.)

Part of the genius of the movie is that while the hunt (Deckard's search for the escaped replicants) proceeds with our full audience approval, we are simultaneously horrified not only by the ethical implications of this massive genetic experiment, but also by the actual *accomplishments* of this scientifically sophisticated society. The movie presents a state of affairs that is as morally abhorrent to us as serving "boiled dog" at a dinner party is to humans in 2019, for whom dogs have become extremely precious because they are so rare. Even Deckard finds that he is acquiring sympathy for his victims.

The novel from which the film was adapted, *Do Androids Dream of Electric Sheep?* makes it much more explicit that the darkness and desolation of *Blade Runner*'s world is due to World War Terminus, which destroyed almost all animal life and has poisoned the air with radiation dust. The movie creates this sense of wasteland through the unremitting darkness, rain, fog, lack of privacy, and images of confinement. The horror is increased as the number of religious references multiplies in the film: the importance of the eye and the value of "seeing" the truth (about a person or a situation; Matthew 6:22-24 NRSV); the pyramidlike shape of the commerce buildings (Egyptian gods); the blotting out of the sun (Revelation 6:12 NRSV); the idea of "meeting your maker" (Hebrews 11:8-10 KJV); the reference to the prodigal son and the waiting father (Luke 15:11-32 NRSV); the nail in Roy's hand that becomes an instrument of Deckard's salvation (Jesus' crucifixion); and the dove that flies into the sky when Roy dies (cf. Matthew 3:16-17 NRSV). There are more.

It is in anger that Roy Batty, leader of the escaped replicants, and his combat team enter Earth—anger at their creator, Tyrell, who has usurped God the Creator's life-giving role. The team members, though they are not human, are grappling with the most elemental of human responses: the fear of death—the fear of extinction that can bring a person near to God in fury or in reverence. Eyes, the "windows to the soul" (from *Secrets & Lies*), betray the replicants' "self"; they also see the wonders of the universe. "You are the prodigal son," Tyrell says to Roy when he sees him; but this is no joyous homecoming for either creature or creator. Roy grieves like Milton's Lucifer in *Paradise Lost*, a magnificent creature born to long for heaven but doomed to rebel and be cast out. Roy blinds his creator in a shattering visual reference to the blinding of Oedipus Rex or the blinding of Gloucester in *King Lear*.

Blade Runner contains multiple religious references, but few comforts. Even the owl we see in Tyrell's office, ancient symbol of wisdom, is artificial. Yet this film nonetheless stimulates profound religious meditation—not simply on issues of ethical responsibility, as mentioned above, but also on what makes a human being precious and inviolable. Contrasted with the perverted model-designs of the false creator Tyrell perched atop his 700-story corporate offices is the divine covenant between the Creator God and human beings that baptizes all of life—the covenant that is born inexplicably when one human being cherishes another as unique and lovable. In this film, love is as mysterious as it has been throughout time. Rachael is the ultimate Other; yet when Deckard reaches out to love her, she becomes a person bound to human life. She becomes authentic, acquiring human nature in response to the love that itself reflects the joy of the Creator.

The Nexus 6 replicants were created with built-in time limitations. The hour and the moment of their deaths are known. But this film, as surely as do *Strangers in Good Company* or *Secrets & Lies*, exposes the tyranny of such clock-driven obsessions as a perversion of the *good* time of God, the Kingdom time where all life and each person is treasured—even Roy Batty, who in his suffering and death has become human. As Deckard watches over the body of his enemy, he weeps; replicant or not, he too at last has become human.

QUESTIONS 1. *Gattaca* (1997), like *Blade Runner,* explores some of the implications of trying to create perfect human beings. We work on fine-tuning prenatal diagnosis; we want perfect children; we want to predict and prevent diseases. In what ways does *Blade Runner* explore the issues of genetic engineering? What kind of person would we wish to create if we had the power? Do you think that Western scientific research is moving us toward "genetic tyranny" (a phrase used by Michael Wilmington in writing about the film world of *Gattaca*)?

2. In *Blade Runner*, the publicity for the offshore worlds speaks of beginning a new life. Why are people leaving Earth for the offshore worlds? What effect do the ads have on your feelings toward emigration and colonization?

3. Rick and Roy are mortal enemies: pursuer and pursued. Nonetheless, although Roy has Rick at his mercy, he saves his life. Why?

4. Is Deckard a replicant? If you think he is, how would you know? Would this make a difference in your response to him as the hero?

Contact
Robert Zemeckis, 1997, 150 min.; PG

This movie is almost as satisfying for the questions it *didn't* ask as for those it *did*. I thought immediately of what needed to be confronted. I went out of the theater not only amazed at the accomplishment of *Contact*'s opening sequence (those two-plus minutes were worth the whole movie) but itching to discuss its problems with someone. To defamiliarize, to disturb—this had been accomplished without gratuitous violence or steamy sex.

PLOT Scientist Ellie Arroway (Jodie Foster) has been reaching out to far places and spaces since childhood. A loving father and a school system more far-seeing than most nurtured her intellectual gifts and stimulated her curiosity; she begins with a ham radio, then branches out into mathematics, computer science, and astronomy. She could teach anywhere she wants to.

What she wishes, however, is to make contact with life-forms in other parts of the universe. She rigorously defends her research before dozens of agencies, hoping to receive funds to continue her work (a hard-hearted government program wants to direct its funds to more "practical" ends). She wins a grant for SETI (Search for Extraterrestrial Intelligence). The desired contact comes, and a massive spacecraft is built. Now everyone wants aboard—almost literally. Ellie is launched to a designated meeting place in the Vega star system.

REFLECTIONS *Contact* crosses the line between the "real" and the imagined, this world and the other. Its opening sequence sucks us into hyperspace, one ball of color exploding into another, all folding back into the human eye of the inquisitive child Ellie. Here we have the blueprint for the entire film. No matter what the story particulars are, we will be transported beyond the limits of human existence into another world through the power of creative imagination, art, and technical expertise—that is, through a movie.

The instrument for this miraculous feat is the eye, which in the film is extended to include the ear (the first contact comes through sound) and touch (one of the main researchers is blind). You might say that this movie's vision exceeds its reach. But its vision is grand—no less than to imagine what lies beyond this earth. No, it is more: to imagine that the message from Beyond (from life-forms presumably more advanced than our own) is that we must hold one another very tightly and keep mystery and faith alive.

What are the questions I wish the film had explored more fully? First, the one introduced when Ellie asks her father if someday she might be able to radio through to her dead mother. "That is beyond our power," he replies simply. Ellie's is a question about life after death, and her search for life elsewhere in the universe is one side of that inquiry. Jodie Foster has commented that Ellie is "searching for some kind of purity, searching for something out there that she can't find here."[19] Far from being mortal enemies, as the film portrays, science and religion are each guided by the quest for truth. Science must be religious at its core; otherwise, it collapses into expediency and power.

A second question raised by the film's story involves the morality of scientific exploration. In *Jurassic Park,* a mathematician (Jeff Goldblum) in the midst of scientists voices concerns about the use and abuse of knowledge. How much should our desire to know and our ability to experiment be restrained by caution? Where do we fit in the chain of evolution? Do we have a right to disrupt or abort natural changes?

Why go to another planet at all? This question is raised in the movie, but only as part of a battle for money between pure research and practical science. What hides beneath the numbers (half a trillion dollars to build the spacecraft, and another half to build its secret double) is the shocking expenditure of funds. What we see from outer space currently is that our ozone layer has been seriously compromised. What we *don't* see is the poverty in many third world countries or the pockets of poverty here in our own American cities and rural areas. Can we imagine mustering the international will to attack poverty with the same zest used to build the spacecraft in *Contact*? Money may not solve problems that are deeply set into societies or economic systems. But in this film, the "nations of the earth" clearly are distracted from even thinking about these problems by the excitement of the building project. It's like a circus.

One of the biggest flaws in the film is its failure to engage in any serious way with the theological dimension of Ellie's search. The carnival atmosphere at the site of the first launching reminds me of the gaggle of religious hucksters assembled to bemoan the approaching end of the world in

On the Beach. Is this the best that religious *practice* (not *faith*) can muster—charlatans or terrorists? Why is Ellie put to the God-test in her interview before the international selection committee—a test to see whether she believes in a small deity hanging out in space somewhere—a god of popular belief, as though polls established the viability of truth? What kind of "God" is implied in the question, "Do you believe in God?"

The answer to this last question is expressed by her smarmy rival, David (formerly Ellie's boss and mentor), in a televised speech that appeals to the most shallow belief possible. David believes in a god of power and will that nonetheless needs its existence proved by an expensive space trip.

This is not the God of the Scriptures, the One who covenants and comforts. This is not a God who prizes gentleness and innocence, who welcomes the shamed.[20] It is a cultural artifact, a cold and shallow idea, manufactured like *Contact*'s elaborate spaceship to fit our own need to dominate one another.

Where is *truth* in this movie? It may lie in the sacred space Ellie enters on Vega. Whether she imagines her trip or actually experiences it is unimportant. She stands face to face with beauty and with her beloved father. Even though I was not satisfied by the sequence that shows her supposed encounter ("contact") with the aliens, I'm not sure how it could have been done differently. To represent what is not known—to picture the invisible—requires an enormous imaginative effort. Other filmmakers handle the unknown with horror. Director Zemeckis at least has the grace to imagine that other life-forms might be benign, might even have healing powers. This is a generous vision.

Ellie is one smart woman, competent and independent but willing to admit, like the ancient, wise women and men, that "I don't know." And in that acknowledgment of the unknown lies her strength.

QUESTIONS 1. *Contact* wants to engage some serious questions, among which is the origin and destiny of the universe. How well do you think the film does this? Where does it succeed, and where does it fail? How might this question be more fully explored?

2. Much is made of Ellie's "atheism." By what standard is she judged an atheist? Do you agree, or do you see her skepticism as part of her desire to believe? Why does the movie make such a point of her lack of religious faith? Is the dialogue helped or hurt by its rigid separation into well-meaning scientists and kooky religious believers? What is director Zemeckis really after with all the talk about belief in God?

3. In *La Femme Nikita,* a movie that exploits audience fascination with stylish violence, the romantic lead is a grocery clerk. In *Secrets & Lies,* the romantic hero is a crab-walking scaffolder. Both these films want us to believe that the only way for persons to learn what it is to be "human" (and to survive in a hazardous world) is to touch and love one another. In *Contact,* the lead is a handsome *theologian* (Matthew McConaughey) who also happens to be an internationally respected religious leader. Does this romance story add to or detract from the film as a whole? How might this part of the story be changed to strengthen our understanding of the meaning of Ellie's space explorations? Does the romantic lead have to be a preacher, or handsome, for instance, or would the movie's point about love be made just as well if he were a thief *(French Kiss)* or a heavy-set jazz musician (Clint Eastwood's marvelous movie about Charlie Parker, *Bird*)?

Chapter 4 explores authenticity and alienation through vocation, the search not only for meaning in life but for a meaningful way to express our gifts. Seen as a specifically religious calling (priest, preacher, rabbi), vocation can bridge perceived gaps between secular and sacred worlds by interpreting the Scriptures and preaching the word of God. In the arena of our daily lives, however, vocation is a concern for each of us, created in the image of God and looking to live and to work not apart from the world but in the middle of it. The secular and the sacred are one realm, where religious values are carried across from one part of our life to another: household, business, health care, politics, liturgy, friendship.

SCENE: 4
TAKE:

VOCATION

Diary of a Country Priest
Wall Street

INTRODUCTION

> ### "Show me the money."
>
> *Professional football player Rod Tidwell, to his sports agent, Jerry Maguire, in* Jerry Maguire

"You complete me" is one of the key lines in the movie *Jerry Maguire*. The competing line, "Show me the money," shouted by the irrepressible running back (Cuba Gooding, Jr.) to his desperate sports agent, Jerry (Tom Cruise), identifies the conflict—meaning versus money—that undercuts Jerry's efforts to find romance, friendship, or mission. Jerry dares to buck the one (money) to find the other (meaning) and discovers that it is difficult to keep those explosive opposites together.

The mission statement Jerry prepares for his company, in which he bravely argues that work should be based on human decency, gets him fired. His part of the corporate world, selling athletes, is fueled not by integrity but by image that serves wealth.

Jerry's struggle begins with a respectable but fairly narrow concern about vocation: how to do what you're good at without compromising basic human values—such as not to sacrifice your client's health or well-being, violate trust, or put dollars before life. How can you keep high ideals (or self-respect) in a money culture, yet still feed yourself?

Over the course of the movie, this question broadens its focus to include issues of vocation as a calling to become a whole person in relationship and covenant. How do we simultaneously care for ourselves and for others? Initially, we wonder whether Jerry will win back his clients and outsmart his scummy rival, Bob Sugar (Jay Mohr), who fired him even though Jerry had been his mentor. (Compare *The Godfather, Wall Street,* and *Donnie Brasco*; betrayal of the mentor is such a frequent thread in contemporary movies that it must reflect some current anxieties.)

Jerry and his sole client are triumphant on the playing field and in the bidding wars. But Jerry discovers that what he needs is not a different job or a new approach to this one—he needs a spiritual transfusion. Finding his vocation in its fullest sense means that he must shift his orientation away from isolation and self-interest to affection, relationship, and community. This he is able to do, once he recognizes that he is "completed" in the love of his friend and his wife.

Jerry's struggles are so firmly anchored in prosperous nineties urban life that it may not be immediately apparent how strongly his story resonates with that of Edna Spaulding (Sally Field) in *Places in the Heart*. Not prosperity, but poverty and destitution hung over Depression-era Texas; not cancellation of health-club membership, but possible starvation was the consequence of losing a job or a husband.

As a widow, Edna inherits the tasks of her tragically murdered husband. This requires that she drastically alter the way she defines her *self*: not as dependent or desperate, but as faithful and open. The line in *Jerry Maguire,* "You complete me," no longer applies just to Edna and her late husband, bound forever in faithful love and trust, but to all the outcasts she embraces in the new household she stitches together after he dies. "You complete me" is what the Hebrew Scriptures call *hesed,* "faithful, responsible love," as Edna takes in the unwanted in this insular Texas town, and *agape* as her love exposes bigotry and lack of charity in the townspeople.

Places in the Heart illuminates vocation and highlights the insights of *Jerry Maguire*. Edna Spaulding is a mother, a widow, a farmer, a boardinghouse keeper, and a nonracist. Each of these characteristics knocks her farther down the scale of respect in her small Texas town. (She is also poor, but so are most of the others.) If she can be represented as a person of dignity whose search for vocation and meaning is critical, then this becomes a model for every person—Jews and Gentiles, slaves and free, men and women (Galatians 3:28). The importance of Edna's story is embodied in the film by the dignity given women, children, African Americans, and those who are blind in a remarkable visual replay of Jesus' dinners with taxpayers and sinners. Power and money have disappeared from the equation.

Neither Edna nor Antonia in *Antonia's Line* (Netherlands, 1995; Academy Award winner for Best Foreign Language Film) would be written up in *The Wall Street Journal*. Neither would my amazing mother nor my Aunt Georgia. My mother used to say, "The children that the other teachers don't want: Those are the ones I love the most." The cleverness and resilience of these women did not have an impact on the major commercial markets. But theirs were Kingdom lives lived in faithful responses to the commands to treat all persons with generosity and charity.

Jerry might get a feature article, but only because in the movie he is successful in promoting a client who has been blacklisted by the powerhouse sports agencies. In the nineties, we love stories about *successful* underdogs. But the heart of Jerry's story, his painful search for an authentic self free to love others—*this* would be ignored. Edna Spaulding's story tells us that the search for authenticity—the desire to bridge alienation and enter community with God and other people—anchors vocation.

REFLECTIONS Hollywood films too often have clouded the picture of vocation. The dominant image is vocation as the perfect job, with money and success as the measures of worth. Mainstream Hollywood movies deliver an ideal that is hard for men to imitate and impossible for most women to crack: the young, handsome hero, powerful in mind and physique—a mover and shaker, a molder and leader of people. Rare is the conflict-driven movie, such as *Platoon* or *Crimson Tide*, that allows—even places into the foreground— ethical questions and moral strength (such as *Tide*'s repeated allusions to Hiroshima and Nagasaki, with the suggestion that nations should always weigh human considerations over technical ones). You are what you do; your identity is wrapped up in your work—this is an idea that persists even though it received such a thorough debunking in *Citizen Kane* (1941) and *It's a Wonderful Life* (1946).

What happens if a person becomes incapacitated through accident, violence, or illness *(Born on the Fourth of July, Regarding Henry, Passion Fish)*? That's the dark question hidden behind the bravado of action movies, a question that rarely surfaces, because it won't boost box-office receipts. When the culture is profit- and product-driven, the weak are at risk.

Vocation, then, has little to do with power; it has to do with naming and being called into relation and community. Vocation surely resembles Ben Frank Moss's meditation when he spoke of his decision to leave theology for painting: "I had been claimed." Through his calling, he has sought to "reclaim a union with the Other through imagination and memory"—to go home. Reorientation of his life is intimately bound with his awakened spiritual life.[1]

This is what Jesus, Paul, and the early church had in mind when they spoke of vocation. Paul defines himself as "called to be an apostle of Christ Jesus by the will of God" (1 Corinthians 1:1 NRSV). It is in this same sense that the author of Hebrews writes of Abraham as one "called to set out for a place that he was to receive as an inheritance" (Hebrews 11:8 NRSV). There is a person or a power who not only names, but summons, and there is a task (to be an apostle) or a gift with responsibilities (to receive an inheritance).

Similarly, Jesus called his disciples to "fish for people" (Matthew 4:19 NRSV). The one who calls has such authority that the person being called must drop everything and reorder his or her life by that command. Edna Spaulding was called, in this sense—called to be nurturer, provider, and, most critically, *lover*, in the sense of the Jesus who ate with lepers, prostitutes, and tax collectors. There is no room and no excuse for racial prejudice or exclusion of the "unfit" in this generous view of the Kingdom.

The two films that follow, *Diary of a Country Priest* and *Wall Street*, come from far different times and cultures—not just in the worlds they show (provincial France; urban New York City), but also in their portrayals of vocation. Controversial director Oliver Stone is a public preacher, pounding home lessons about Americans' irresponsibility in Vietnam *(Platoon)* or our addiction to violence *(Natural Born Killers)*. His lesson in *Wall Street* is similar to that of *Jerry Maguire*, except it is darker: The love of money corrupts; human happiness comes before profits. We have a public responsibility—a vocation—to support and not corrupt one another. Vocation in *Wall Street* has much to do with authenticity and integrity (responsibility to ourselves) and *hesed* (care for others). *Wall Street* introduces many issues of private and public morality.

In *Diary*, Robert Bresson relentlessly probes the theological nature of life's challenges. If vocation is a calling, how do we know who calls us? How can we believe in a divine being or divine will when so much we see challenges our faith? By what standard can the good and faithful life be judged? I begin with *Diary of a Country Priest*, because its style, its honesty, and its attempts to answer these questions are critical to understanding the deeper meanings of vocation as we have begun to probe them in this chapter.

GOING TO THE MOVIES

Diary of a Country Priest
Robert Bresson, France, 1950, 116 min.; Not Rated

Diary of a Country Priest is a challenging film. Group response to public viewings has ranged from the boredom of a high-school group accustomed to rapid-fire action flicks, to the thoughtful perceptions of a graduate-school class of mixed ages and backgrounds, to the rapt and enthusiastic attention to its nuances by an auditorium full of French undergraduates. A mixed group of French academics and townsfolk found it intriguing though pessimistic, while an American audience praised its formal beauty, its innovative and meaningful use of sound, and its attention to the complexity of religious belief and religious symbolism. (Interestingly, this was a secular audience.)

Diary's tough viewing—and its appeal—have nothing to do with the time in which it was made (1950) or its country of origin (France, a nation of cinema lovers). It is a work of genius, like its director's *Pickpocket* (1959), an adaptation of *Crime and Punishment*; and like Carl Dreyer's *Ordet* and *Day of Wrath*. Its theological interest stems only partially from its use of a priest as the hero. This movie takes seriously such issues as faith and doubt, sexuality, integrity, and vocation. It grapples intensely with the definition of *grace*.

PLOT A young priest, fresh out of seminary, takes his first parish. He makes all the mistakes made by young clergy. He is overzealous, intellectual, and intense; he worries about God and the welfare of his parishioners. He makes a few friends—the Curé de Torcy, a priest from a neighboring village; and Dr. Delbende, the local physician. Unfortunately, Delbende commits suicide. The parish responds to his ministry and his misery with censure, hostility, and shunning.

As his miseries compound, the young priest finds that he can no longer pray; he feels that God has deserted him. Moreover, he suffers from cancer of the liver, which allows him to digest only bread and wine. Somehow, he finds the strength to speak the words of truth to the most alienated persons in his parish: the Countess and her daughter Chantal. The young priest dies in a garret, but not before he has ridden on a motorcycle and visited with the mistress of his old friend from seminary days.

REFLECTIONS When I recently watched *Contact* again, I was struck by its resemblance to *Diary of a Country Priest*. Among *Contact*'s other story features, it tells of an astronomer's faith journey. Its dazzling opening sequence, a whipping blast of interlaced, colored particles, sets a mood of excitement and expectation of the unknown. So does *Diary*'s opening: A simple road sign for Ambricourt, the young priest's destination, is superimposed upon his face, forming the shadow of a cross.

As *Contact* builds toward an encounter with extraterrestrial beings on Vega, so also does *Diary* build toward a "contact," a vision of truth. In *Contact*, Ellie Arroway's progress is stained by deaths, aborted projects, and official duplicity, including betrayals by her former mentor and her former sweetheart; in *Diary* the young priest's path increasingly acquires the marks of the Way of the Cross—persecutions and almost certainly an obscure death.

What motivates Ellie's quest? The irresistible pull of science, but more, the shameful absurdity of death. What does she learn from her journey to Vega? That the "other world" is home. The face of God is the face of those whom you love: for her, the face of her dead father. The "beyond" is not horror; it is beauty, love, and trust. Ellie is forced to admit faith and mystery into her life. These are splendid, ancient, biblical truths. Yet I was puzzled. Perhaps the director of *Contact* made a mistake in trying to make visible the invisible. How do you picture God?[2]

It is here that *Diary* excels as art and as a religious film. For the young priest's visions, we see only a black screen. We know what he *thinks* he has seen: the Virgin Mary; his mother; and a child with work-roughened hands. We don't need to see the images; our mind does the work. It is odd that in cinema—an art that depends on giving you things to look at—the most powerful images are often the ones called up by your own mind.

The priest's visions are preceded by a series of encounters with the people in his parish and followed by his spiritual awakening and his death. We will examine the visions first, and then return to one of the key encounters in the movie that opens the way to the priest's spiritual enlightenment.

The priest, obviously ill, has staggered out into a stormy night after one of his interminable parish visits. We see his figure silhouetted against the poplar tree where, earlier in the film, he had imagined his parish members were crucifying him. (He has been experiencing a cruel reception in this, his first parish.) The priest falls, dying to his old life and experiencing a mystical vision. He "sees" truth, beauty, and the meaning of history. His own history is part of this. His childhood poverty is acknowledged and sanctified. The body of God (here, clearly linked with the Maternal, the Ancient Truth) is a real, physical body, not the disembodied "soul" of the Greeks. How can we know God? By looking into the faces of the earth's creatures, even the poor, even women, even the stained.

When the priest awakens, he sees Seraphita, a poor, devious young girl on the edge of womanhood, who has been one of his persecutors. She is represented not as an ideal woman, not as a temptress, but as a rescuer. She cleans his face of the blood he has vomited—the discharge of his disintegrating body—which she curiously likens to "blackberries," that sweet fruit of a ripe summer. She is accustomed, she says flatly, to tending cows and to cleaning up vomit and filth. She wipes his face clean with caring hands. It is she who represents the Virgin Mary; the child of God; one who has been with us since the beginning of the world; a goddess of the ancient world—ever-present as with the other men and women of the priest's life in the world of work and suffering.[3]

The language in this sequence is deliberately inclusive. The woman with work-roughened hands is both *this* child and the Virgin, but she is also the priest's own mother, whose hands were so callused by chores that she could no longer turn the pages of her volume of *The Imitation of Christ*.

The priest's visions clarify all that has gone before in the movie. In particular, they anchor in faith the ethical spin put on the priest's ministry when he encounters the doubting Countess in one of *Diary*'s key sequences. (When director Bresson prepared the final version of *Diary*, he cut out about thirty minutes of film, mostly interactions of the priest with his parishioners. He kept *this* sequence, though, and it is powerful.) By the time the young priest enters the Countess's sitting room at her manor house, he has suffered a series of devastating setbacks in his ministry. His friend, Delbende, the local doctor (who had seen in the questing young priest a younger version of himself), has killed himself from despair. The young priest is ill and feels God has deserted him.

The interview with the Countess begins disastrously. The priest has come to confront her with her daughter Chantal's dangerous situation. Headstrong and despairing, distressed by her father's infidelity and her mother's coldness, Chantal may take her own life simply to revenge herself on her parents. What began as a pastoral call by a weak and inexperienced young man takes a startling turn. The priest suddenly goes into pastoral overdrive: He says what he is really thinking rather than comforting his haughty parishioner with smooth words.

The subject is no less than that of the Psalms and the Gospels: How should we respond in the face of unbearable loss and suffering—in the Countess's case, the death of her beloved baby son? Can we see and rejoin the dead? Where and what is *heaven*? Will we see God face to face and know the truth? Will we finally be able to judge right from wrong?

The Countess's attitude toward suffering and loss is the same as Dr. Delbende's had been: defiance of a malevolent or absent God. If there is no God, then my life is meaningless. If there is a God, then the death of my little child is a horror. There are no more important questions than these. The Countess's anguish began with the death of her child and her dead marriage and ended with hatred for God.

But God's goodness and love are not "proved" by our happiness and prosperity, the priest counsels; we cannot know the unknown. To blame God for the death of your baby son is to assume that the universe is hostile; to wish that everything were ordered to our desires is to assume the same.

Through the priest's daring and spontaneous confrontation with this embittered and grieving woman, he faces his own fury at a life too quickly ended—even with the horror of his own starved and abused childhood, which we guess from Dr. Delbende's cryptic comments when he examines the priest. For a moment, I believe, the Countess becomes the priest's own mother, born into poverty, not wealth, and worn to an early death as a charwoman. The priest is, like Frank in *Sling Blade*, the little son the mother could not save. When the priest confronts the Countess, he faces both his dead mother and himself. How should we respond to intractable evil? He offers the ancient words: "Thy kingdom come, thy will be done on earth"—acceptance of suffering and death as the human condition, while remaining actively engaged in God's work in the world.

In *Diary*, we could easily construct a glorification of servitude. The materials are all there—the priest's suffering mother, the suffering Christ, and the clever and worldly wise Seraphita. The mistress of the priest's old seminary buddy (who cleans houses to support her tubercular lover) seems to be one more willing victim. She has refused to marry her lover, she confides, so that she will not ruin his chance to return to the priesthood.

But we should resist the temptation to glorify the servitude of women or the suffering visited on women and men by an unjust social order. This is not what the priest experiences in his vision of holiness. He sees rather the generosity of the woman's offering of herself and recognizes her as God's hands here on earth. She becomes the agent of reconciliation for the priest, the person who reveals to him the sanctity of vocation—not one set apart from the world, but one composed of rich, earthy elements: the love of man and woman, the adventure of friendship, and even the priest's own doubts and physical collapse.

The priest has returned "home" through this woman with work-roughened hands, home to his mother, whose faith infused her life. This does not represent a stagnation or reversion to his early life, but rather the advent of *new* life. The priest is a changed person who has taken in the whole world. His parting words are,

"All is grace" — grace as charity, grace as the kingdom of God that exists within the daily life of our imperfect world.

QUESTIONS 1. Late in the film, the priest is given a ride on a motorcycle. What meaning does this event — and the conversation he has with Olivier, the owner of the cycle — have for him?

2. What does Dr. Delbende mean when he tells the priest they are of the "same race"? How does the priest interpret these words? What impact does the old doctor's suicide have on the younger man?

3. What stages does the priest go through as he tries to come to terms with his vocation? How do these intersect with his growing feeling that he is, in his life, a "prisoner of the Holy Agony"?

4. To what extent does the priest have freedom of choice in his life? How might he have responded differently to the demands of his parish? Would this have made any difference in the parishioners' attitudes toward him? Do you observe any similarities between the workings of this parish and your own congregation? Are certain difficulties built into community life?

Wall Street
Oliver Stone, 1987, 126 min.; R

Wall Street differs from *Diary of a Country Priest,* but it plays a similar tune: A young man goes out into the world to seek himself and his vocation, is tempted, and comes to himself.[4] Directors Bresson and Oliver Stone both are on a mission: to present the world as they see it, and to shake up their spectators. Where Bresson heightens religious awareness and is also much more attentive to the roles and voices of women, Stone's purpose seems more pointedly political—no less than to urge Americans to look long and hard at their misconstrual of "vocation" as making and moving money.

PLOT Charlie Sheen plays Bud Fox, an aspiring young stockbroker, ambitious but naive. Persistence gets him the attention of Gordon Gekko (Michael Douglas), high-stakes stock market player, who tutors Bud in the ways and wiles of big-money capitalism. Gekko is persuasive; Bud, right-minded but eager to rise above his blue-collar background, caves in when he begins to see profits. (One of my preacher friends once explained why he had left the ministry for the stock market: "I got tired of wearing threadbare suits.")

Bud has a dream: to "be on the other side"—not powerless and passive, but a big man who controls others' lives—a Gordon Gekko. Bud begins to drink, smoke, and accept women as bargaining chips. Finally, he sees the light, uses his new-found smarts to outwit Gekko, and brings down Gekko's empire. He also gets himself, Gekko, and his friend busted by the Securities and Exchange Commission (SEC), which doesn't react too favorably to insider trading.

REFLECTIONS Bud is a young man who longs for greatness. In traditional stories, such a man is provided with a mentor: Odysseus has his old friend, Mentor *(The Odyssey)*, and Luke Skywalker has Obi-wan (Ben) Kenobi *(Star Wars)*. Bud's father, Carl, and Gordon Gekko present him with contrasting definitions of vocation, including those nonprofitable virtues such as integrity and compassion— virtues his father embodies with his whole life. Vocation, Bud finds, is more complicated than stockbroker versus blue-collar worker, the only alternatives he initially thinks are open to him.

Wall Street is structured as a Manichaean (dualistic) drama—a morality play with Good (Bud's father) on one side, and Evil (Gekko) on the other.[5] Bud, caught between the two, must choose where his allegiance lies.[6] He sells out his father's company through insider information, tempts his best friend to break the law, and works inhuman hours. But he is becoming rich. Profit replaces integrity, relationship, and charity in Bud's new definition of *vocation*.

Who will save him? Is this meant to be a melodrama with a last-minute rescue and a happy ending? Oliver Stone complicates the Good/Evil opposition by portraying Gordon Gekko as pragmatic rather than purely evil. Gekko plays on other people's weaknesses; further, as he argues, he is not doing something new, he simply does what other people do, only much better. Stone's target is much larger than just one man—it is commodity culture itself, the culture of Harold C. Simmons: "Business acumen and bold timing, backed up by swarms of lawyers telling how far to the inch he could push, propelled [Simmons] into the ranks of the nation's billionaires. . . . [He] built his fortune making takeover raids on undervalued companies."[7]

The centerpiece of the film is Gekko's speech to one company's stockholders, during which he turns a hostile audience into a friendly one. The moment is critical: Not only does he have to sway the company's little investors, he has to vanquish their officers, keep Bud on his side, and maintain the good press that has bolstered his financial empire. All this he does in a speech that could have been crafted by the ancient master of rhetoric himself, Cicero, whose guidelines have taught speechwriters for two thousand years to "convince others to act the way we want them to." "What are the desires of my audience? How can I motivate them to do my will? How shall

I disguise my weakest arguments? How to dazzle my listeners so they are no longer able to reason matters through independently?"[8]

Gekko plays on his audience's weaknesses—not only their desire to maximize profits, but also their ignorance, even though they live in a culture of mass media and mass advertising, of the power of language to move and persuade. Gekko's task is to convince his audience not only that "greed is good" but that "good is greed." He redefines terms. Greed is usually connected with the proscription against covetousness; it is one of the deadly sins in the medieval pantheon of nasty vices.

Gekko turns ideas based on the great religious traditions upside down. Righteousness in the Hebrew Scriptures and Jesus' teachings such as the Sermon on the Mount is oriented toward the powerless and friendless, the marginalized. Not money, but the love of money—*greed*—is the root of all evil. Now, says Gekko, "evolution" and "progress" have supplanted old ideas that hold back profits. Pulling out a commonly known and accepted idea, he continues: "Greed captures the essence of the evolutionary spirit."

The *mise-en-scène* in this sequence favors Gekko. Unlike the company's leaders, who are pinned behind their big table and podium and are mostly viewed at medium to long distance or from behind, Gekko moves in and around his audience, hand in pocket like an ordinary working man. The camera moves with him, shooting him in a variety of close-ups or medium shots. We are treated to close shots of Bud's and Gekko's attractive, young supporters. Because we have identified with Bud, we too can be seduced by Gekko's speech.

Gekko is like an itinerant preacher, taking a line and spinning it out: "I'm going to take this airline and turn it around." Cleverly twisting word meanings, he takes the negative load of "greed" and turns it around to mean "promise." Greed is right; greed works; greed clarifies.

Gekko sets up his case: "America is a second-rate power." This puts the argument on national turf. The American flag flies dutifully in the background. Anything you'd do to hold a company back would be an act of disloyalty to your country, he implies. Survival of the fittest becomes the means of saving the company and saving the country; therefore, greed will save both.

The religious language plays with the audience's worst fears and anxieties. Once the audience accepts Gekko's basic premises (and we see that they do), then he becomes a *messiah* who will *save* them by the power of greed! Profit is enthroned as the greatest good and thus replaces God. The exchange of terms, greed for good for God, is complete.

The problems embedded in this speech are legion and must be examined if we are to understand Bud's actions after this crucial public speech. Gekko claims to be a liberator, on the side of the little person against the overpaid leaders. Among the ironies of this premise is that he is far richer than the company's leaders, yet he pretends to be just another ordinary guy. Further, shareholders are not really little people either; the little people are the workers and their wives and children. Few of these stockholders will suffer from changes in the company's financial status. None of them would be ruined if its stock dropped.

An underlying problem in this and Gekko's other business deals is that the deals are inherently heartless, removed from any connection to the lives of the persons who are served or the persons whose past and future are bound up in the businesses. Gekko never touches anything made in his investment companies. Certainly, he is far from attachment to the land or means of survival. He is a parasite, living off air, other people's blood, and wire money transfers.

Knowledge is the key to making money; in *Wall Street*, it's knowledge gained from relationships and trust betrayed, a predatory rather than benevolent use of knowledge. The film echoes Genesis, point after point: How will you live your life? Will you cherish or consume other people?

Embedded in the movie's structure and central to its comprehensive understanding of vocation is the central question of *value*. Two definitions given are these: first, "that amount of some commodity, medium of exchange . . . which is considered to be an equivalent for something else; a fair or adequate equivalent return"; and second, "Ethics. That which is worthy of esteem for its own sake; that which has intrinsic worth." The quotation given is strikingly appropriate: "Everyone is in danger of valuing himself for what he does."[9]

How shall we reorient our perspective on vocation? By recognizing that it is thoroughly anchored in both our spiritual journey and this world. Vocation is not something that belongs to a dirty and inherently evil workaday world, nor does it need to be defined as a "religious" job. It is of one piece, the calling of the person in responsible community. Jerry Maguire doesn't need to give up his profession as a sports agent to change his life. He doesn't need a new job; he needs a new heart.

QUESTIONS 1. Bud, who comes to himself like the biblical Prodigal Son (Luke 15:11-32), realigns with his father and uses his new manipulative skills to ruin Gekko. The toppling of Gekko's great empire is carefully orchestrated as the victory of David over Goliath, the little person over the mighty. But it still requires that one friend betray another. Does the film play off one set of moral values (honesty, family loyalty, biblical commandments) against another (friendship, trust)?

2. Bud and Gekko move money by computer, by phone, by wire. The manipulation of assets, shares, and power is not the same as driving the corn to market (as my

grandfather drove on his wagon in Texas), where some relation exists between your skill as a farmer and the product you have grown. Does it matter what's sold and to whom you are selling it?

3. This movie appeared in 1987, anticipating the falls of a number of prominent stock market manipulators. How well has the film aged? Does it ring true to what we know about current practices in American (and world) business? How has the rapid development of communications technology altered the business scene? Are some of the issues addressed in this film (the gap between management and workers, for instance) under discussion?

4. "The capital accumulation that made the industrial revolution in England and western Europe possible was derived in large part from colonialism. The regions thus depleted of their wealth were rendered impoverished and dependent."[10] Rosemary Ruether is not the only writer to refer to the dark side of colonialism, which has created the strange situation of having whole countries dedicated to raising crops such as sugar *not* to feed its inhabitants, but to satisfy the tastes of consumers. How does *Wall Street* address this side of consumer culture?

Integrity has multiple dimensions: personal, social, spiritual. It threads its way as a concern through movies of all times and places. Within the boundaries of the Western, however, integrity can be either praised as a virtue or promoted as a false substitute for religious covenant. As we will see, the Western offers an imaginative arena where morality and ethics—the particular expressions of integrity—can be severely tested. Does integrity include charity, responsibility, and stewardship—charity toward native Americans, responsibility to protect the vulnerable, stewardship of natural resources? Does integrity embrace the divine covenant to do justice for all peoples?

SCENE: 5
TAKE:

INTEGRITY

The Searchers
Unforgiven
Lone Star

INTRODUCTION

"I've never run from anybody before."

Marshall Will Kane, in
High Noon

The appearance of Garry Wills's book about John Wayne has opened up forbidden territory in American hero-worship.[1] Wayne began to soar in the 1950s as the embodiment of the supreme rugged individualist, explorer, conqueror, and purifier—a strong, silent saint who carried on his broad shoulders America's obsessions with idealized versions of its past. Wills advances the case that this image—

Wayne as an American icon bigger than life and twice as real—was entirely fabricated by master Hollywood director John Ford to play to the dreams (and anxieties) of a nation ill at ease with its own past.

Most Americans are less than familiar with the particulars of that past. Even if a student can read well enough to get through the eleventh grade in high school, there is still no guarantee that he or she will ever be engaged in tough discussions about the meaning of Manifest Destiny or the impact on the nation of the closing of the frontier or the near-extermination of the country's native population.[2] Hollywood movie studios have busied themselves trying to take care of the possible deficits in our education. Between 1903 and 1967, they churned out thousands of Westerns, beginning with *The Great Train Robbery* in 1903.

The Hollywood Western reveals that in America, the mythic patterns of most cultures have been reversed. There is no exact equivalent for the "social hearth, a temple, a holy city"; New York, Los Angeles, and Chicago are to be fled as places of crime and corruption, not cherished as centers of spiritual refuge like Paris or London. Wills writes: "There is no more defining note to our history than the total absence of a sacred city in our myths. We never had a central cultic place," the result, perhaps, of our insistence that church and state be separate. The American hero lives not in the "temple of the gods," but out on the frontier. Furthermore, he (almost always a *he*) is an outsider,

> a displaced person—arrived from a rejected past, breaking into a glorious future, on the move, fearless himself, feared by others, a killer but cleansing the world of things that "need killing," loving but not bound down by love, rootless but carrying the Center in himself, a gyroscopic direction-setter, a traveling norm.[3]

This is a fearsome description of the American hero, but it captures the spirit of the myth that compelled millions of people from all over the globe to board crowded, barely seaworthy vessels and cross the ocean to these shores.

It also sums up the basic plot lines of the majority of thousands of Western movies. In real life Americans (present and past) may cave in to conformity, but their *dream* has been to live free in mind and body. With that image of freedom comes a ready-made system of ethics that could have come straight out of a medieval knight's moral handbook or the Trojan warrior Hector's code of honor. At the top of the list of Western virtues (the behavior that characterizes a *vir*, Latin for "man") is "integrity." As Wills writes, "The true Western hero is the true American . . . a decent man who will not give up or cheat. He keeps his word. And he will finish what he started."[4]

Many movie fans think of *High Noon* as the quintessential Western. However, Clint Eastwood's *High Plains Drifter* may come closer to a theological vision of the West, with its commingling of good and evil and the complicity of towns in the persecution of its saints. In *Big Guns Talk: The Story of the Western*, Clint Eastwood says that this film is a "What-If story." What if the marshal played by Gary Cooper in *High Noon* had not been able to win out against the villains (his friends all having deserted him)? What if he had been killed, with the tacit or active help of the townspeople—an idea (collective vengeance) that Agatha Christie explores in the mystery novel *Murder on the Orient Express*.[5]

In reality, evil is not confined to one diabolical presence but may be hatched and perpetuated by quite ordinary folk. *High Plains Drifter* is painful to watch, but it faces the problem of the West head-on: Removed from the restraints of legal and communal culture, people may do things they would not dare do if they were surrounded by neighbors, family, and the law. ("The high plains drifter rides into . . . such a town, now plagued by evil and its own guilt.")[6]

REFLECTIONS What is *integrity*? For the Greeks, it meant fulfillment of purpose. For the Hebrews, it meant wholeness, *shalom*, being of one piece. The dictionary defines it as "soundness of moral principle; the character of uncorrupted virtue, especially in relation to truth and fair dealing; uprightness, honesty, sincerity."[7] Yet as it is commonly used in Westerns, integrity seems to mean inner strength and purposefulness that travels with the man rather than being attached to any religion or civilization. Herein may lie a problem: We need to know what that purpose is. It is not the purpose itself that makes integrity a word of praise. There is a difference between the country priest's devotion to doing God's work in the world *(Diary of a Country Priest)* and Gordon Gekko's dedication in *Wall Street* to make money regardless of the cost to human happiness and security.

It may not even be possible to discuss integrity apart from reference to an external source of value. In the Bible, "wholeness" comes from being part of the covenant with the Lord God; it accompanies a community *for whom* and *to whom* one is responsible. When this idea is linked with the American West, "integrity" becomes a particularlt elusive and chameleonic concept.

GOING TO THE MOVIES

The Searchers
John Ford, 1956, 119 min.; Not Rated

Director John Ford, whatever his personal failings (and Garry Wills suggests he had many), understood not only the marketability of "integrity" and the American myth in which the idea was imbedded, but also the morally dark underside of both ideal and myth. Integrity as a quality, limited in its definition to "singleness of purpose" or "shifting moral behaviors," was insufficient to describe what happened to men and women when they were taken from their home environment and transposed to a new land. *The Searchers* is a movie that questions the elevation of integrity as a quality of being that defines "doing the right thing" by the self alone — the self as guided only by survival instinct, intuition, or revenge, not by obligation or allegiance to a higher power.

PLOT Ethan Edwards (John Wayne) returns to his brother's Texas ranch four years after the end of the Civil War. After a brief reunion with his brother, his brother's wife Martha (whom Ethan loves), and their three children, Ethan and some neighbors are decoyed away from the homestead to follow some cattle rustlers. When Ethan returns, he discovers that Comanches have burned the house and killed the family. The two girls have been kidnapped. Soon, Ethan finds the body of the older sister.

Ethan and Martin, a young man who had been adopted by Martha's family, set out to find and rescue the youngest child, Debbie, whom they believe is still alive. Martin foolishly accompanies Ethan rather than staying behind to marry his sweetheart.

Ethan's archenemy is the Comanche chief Scar, who, according to Ethan, is one more thievin', murderin', no-good scoundrel. Scar, however, is Ethan's mirror image. Like Ethan, Scar's family members have been murdered, and he is wedded to revenge. Like Scar, Ethan is bent on the wholesale destruction not only of individual criminals but of all persons who lie outside his own culture.

We see Ethan's and Scar's worlds through Martin's eyes. Director Ford finally gives us romance and a wedding after a long and savage dissection of revenge.

REFLECTIONS *The Searchers* is a deeply troubling film. It plays with the myths of the Western genre; plays with common dramatic conflicts between church and private conscience, or enshrined law and vigilante justice; and plays with basic narrative patterns. The landscape is majestic; visual images often contradict what the characters say. History is used for the setting, but it is reinterpreted as much by what is shown or what is not said as what we think we know.

Most disturbingly, the film is filled with ethnic groups stereotyped not only by their speech and their person (their faces and their dress) but also by Ethan Edwards's running commentary on them. It would be easy today to interpret *The Searchers* through the filter of the Gulf War, "Star Wars" defense technology, the Evil Empire, the Vietnam War, or the Cold War—events that exist in time, but also events that were created and perpetuated in part by rhetoric—talk aimed to influence. Yet it is ultimately frustrating to blame John Ford and those gorgeous sweeping vistas of the Southwest for creating the mentality responsible for military cost overruns and the Cold War—or for racism, which in this film is thoroughly discredited.[8]

However, it is useful to think of the manner in which the Civil War is used as a historical reference and symbol in this film. Ford set the drama in Texas, which fought on the side of the Confederacy, rather than choosing a free state or a new territory (which by extension would have been free when the war started). Thus Ethan wears a "Johnny Reb" coat (which his beloved Martha strokes tenderly, as we see through the open bedroom door in one of the early scenes of the movie). We find out from his captain/preacher that he wasn't around for the surrender: "Don' believe in no surrender." He is an embittered survivor of a war that scorched the South and killed off a high percentage of young men on both sides of the Mason-Dixon line. Ethan stands for a way of life that he believes must not be relinquished.

What is that way of life, exactly? Ethan arrives on the scene as a man of mystery, one element of the Western myth, with a troubled and no doubt violent past. His former captain, now the local preacher, hints that many descriptions of wanted criminals fit Ethan. His family members comment ingenuously, if the war was over four years ago, why didn't he come home before now? He has piles of gold, "fresh-minted." The opening song nostalgically croons, "What makes a man to roam, far away from home?" in its simple, artless cowboy way, keeping both the roaming and the time in the back of our minds. We are cued to guess that Ethan deserted the Army and roamed around at loose ends after the war, robbing the Union pay train and committing other crimes against the men who remained his enemies long after 1865.[9]

Ethan's unsettled life is a "free" life. He views himself as a leader set above the law by nature of his superior endowments; crimes and cruelty alike are justified by his inner code. His is also a life thoroughly poisoned by hatred—not only of Native Americans, Mexicans, and Jews, but also of those less intelligent, strong, or "cool" than he is. It is, for the space of this movie, a life focused on vengeance—not so much vengeance for the scalping of Martin's mother (who may have been Ethan's sweetheart) a quarter-century before, but vengeance for all the impediments that he imagines restrict his complete freedom. Ethan projects his own evil onto the Comanches. In his own twisted mind, they are nothing more than brutal killers, and he fails to see them as a people who are suffering the loss of their land, their freedom, their customs, and their lives.

Ford's most effective questioning of vigilante justice is accomplished almost entirely through Martin, Ethan's sidekick, "he who follows." Martin maintains the supposed goal of their mission, to rescue Debbie. He does not endorse massacre, and he cries when he sees a murdered Comanche woman called Look, saying "She never done nothing to nobody." Ethan, hoping to infect Martin with his own rage, pulls out the clincher, telling Martin that Scar is wearing the scalp of Martin's mother (and therefore must be hunted down to the death). Martin puts this in proper perspective: "That don't change nothin'." Throughout the movie, Martin finds it a more difficult task to prevent Ethan from killing Debbie, a whole herd of buffalo, and all the indigenous peoples in Texas than to survive five long years of cold and starvation.

The seemingly romantic and benign myth of the Western, where killing is justified in the name of some greater goal, is thoroughly undercut here by Ethan's repeated violations of basic human decency. He shoots a thief in the back. He tries to destroy the enemy's food supply. He shoots out the eyes of a dead Comanche to prevent the warrior from entering the spirit world. Martin and the other men in the posse are appalled by Ethan's actions.

The final assault on the emotional power of the myth occurs when Ethan tries to kill Debbie, the person he had given five years of two lives (his own and Martin's) to save. Why? For all the reasons he has revealed previously: Because he feels that Indians are no-good, thieving, brutal, stupid savages who are less than human, and because Debbie has been polluted by living among them. Ethan pretends to be searching for a holy grail (to punish evildoers), but it is a grail that is poisoned by his own hatred. The fact that Debbie survives, the fact that when Ethan catches up with her a second time he lifts her up and returns her home, is due to the grace and strength of Martin (who ironically may be Ethan's own son), a "half-breed" representative of the best that America will become.

QUESTIONS 1. *The Searchers* is repeatedly named as one of the "greatest American movies," appearing, for instance, on the first National Film Registry list prepared by the National Film Preservation Board for the preservation of our national heritage. Yet it presents a national icon, John Wayne, as a character who is hate-filled, disloyal, bigoted, and hell-bent on vengeance. Is it possible that some viewers might see Ethan's opinions and actions as praiseworthy rather than despicable? How does the director guard against this misinterpretation?

2. Critics often remark on the importance of doorways and entrances in the movie, particularly in the opening and closing scenes. In what ways — social, cultural, or moral — do doorways function in this film? How is it important who is inside and who is outside?

3. Ethan treats young Martin with disrespect, even contempt, yet he travels five years with him and wills his possessions to him. What do you make of this? How might this relate to Ethan's ambivalent feelings toward his sworn enemies, the Comanches, and his shadowy past?

4. What is the ultimate attitude of the movie to Manifest Destiny — in this case the movement of white people toward the West and their consequent displacement of the indigenous populations?

Unforgiven
Clint Eastwood, 1992, 131 min.; R

As a work of narrative art, *Unforgiven* both tells a story (William Munny's return to gunfighting) and is a story *about* stories (replays of the myths embodied in Westerns). It is at the same time a tribute to the vitality of the genre and a merciless dissection of that genre. Director Clint Eastwood is acutely aware not only of the particulars in the tradition, but also of the power of the myth to express the longings and the tensions of a people on the move and on the make.

The familiar elements of the genre are almost all there—the corrupt sheriff, the false gunman, the good gunfighter, the comrade, the apprentice, the good-hearted "saloon girls" (prostitues), the shady saloon-keeper. Although Munny's wife, who represents the woman of good reputation, is dead, she is nonetheless a powerful player in the unfolding drama. As one character intones, "He ain't got no wife" (as symbol of civilizing force, a restraint on sex and violence), "at least not one that's above ground."

PLOT It is Kansas, 1880. Hog farmer William Munny (Clint Eastwood), a reformed gunfighter, receives a visit from The Schofield Kid, who proposes that they set out for Wyoming to avenge the mutilation of a young prostitute (and to claim the thousand-dollar reward offered by the other prostitutes). Will reluctantly accepts and recruits his former partner, Ned (Morgan Freeman), in the mission.

Big Whiskey, Wyoming, where the attack had taken place, is ruled by a tyrannical sheriff, Little Bill (played by the six-foot, four-inch Gene Hackman), who runs his town by his own concept of justice. He nearly beats Will to death, suspecting that he is a vigilante (Will is too ill to resist). Little Bill also beats, imprisons, and exiles English Bob, a self-styled "legendary" gunslinger who arrives in town complete with his own chronicler, ready to claim the prostitutes' reward money.

Will and The Kid kill the offending cowboys. Ned bows out of the game, saying that no reward money is worth killing another person. Nonetheless, Little Bill catches up with Ned before he can make it back to Kansas and whips him until he dies.

The murder of his friend transforms Will from a reformed, reflective father and farmer into the killing machine of his own legendary past. He purges the town of evil and rides off into the darkness.

REFLECTIONS Director Eastwood is aware of the visual history and formulaic features of the Western and plays on this awareness in every scene in *Unforgiven*, either embracing a classic camera set-up to create a mood (the long, gold horizon of the opening, complete with shack, clothesline, tree, and gravestone — Frontier America) or exploding audience expectation by the introduction of startling elements to grate against our memory of similar scenes. To accuse Eastwood of lifting plots off earlier movies such as *Shane* is to miss Eastwood's harsh criticism of the legends of the Old West (as well as their violent reality) and his "thorough understanding of his own persona" in *Unforgiven*.[10]

For instance, the obligatory ride of (male) comrades so neatly parodied in *Three Amigos* is returned to "realism." What do men really talk about on those long, womenless rides while straddling a horse? Why, sex, of course, and masturbation. The campfire sessions are stripped of glamour. What is really discussed? Disease and death — the constant companions of lonely men on the trail, drenched relentlessly as they try to sleep, far away from their families and their comfortable beds. The campfire is not the huge, hot one we remember from dozens of ordinary Westerns, but a pitiful, bright patch, foreground left, not enough to keep the men warm or dry or even to light their faces.

Equally, the several saloon confrontations recall and recast saloon scenes from *Shane* and *High Noon*. The first time Will enters Greeley's saloon in Big Whiskey, he does not respond to his taunters with violence — not because he is nobly self-restraining or not interested in fighting, but because he is ill and his gunpowder is wet (and also because he is under the influence of his dead wife).

The constant echoes of other Westerns may delight film buffs, who will pick up references to *Stagecoach*, *High Noon*, and many other classics. But *Unforgiven* is created in such a way that even a novice to movie-watching can quickly understand the premises that underscore the film. The text that flashes onscreen at the beginning provides bare background for this particular tale: "She was a comely young woman and not without prospects," who, to her mother's sorrow, married a "known thief and murderer."

The time and the place for the continuation of Will's story are revealed. When The Schofield Kid first appears at Will's farm, he delivers a short lesson on the myth of the Western hero. He recounts for Will the various *stories* he has heard from his Uncle Pete about Will's exploits, stories that Will either does not remember or has chosen to forget: "Are you are the same Will Munny who . . . " Will responds: "I ain't like that any more. My wife, she—cured me of that. Cured me of drinkin' and wickedness." With great economy, this exchange provides us with *fabula* details—except that many of them are exaggerated or wrong, story-tellings that satisfy the needs of the myth and fit the teller's fantasies but may not have happened.

Through every movement in the partnership of old hand and young apprentice, The Kid serves as a reflector of those legends, serving up variations of old ones and introducing new ones, always contrasting Will's present behavior with what emotions or actions Will, as a hero of a certain kind of myth, ought to display. The lines of the legend are these: This is a cold-hearted, ruthless, fearless man who has killed without remorse or reason. "You was the meanest . . . on account of you're as cold as the snow. You don't have no weak nerve." The Kid himself tries to mold his own behavior according to these versions of the Western myth.[11] "Gon' kill a coupla nogood cowboys," he announces as the purpose of his mission, as though killing is justified if the victims are evil (bountyhunters or mutilators of women).

Will and his former partner, Ned, themselves play endless variations on those themes (death, greed, violence), questioning in their own storytelling not only whether they did what it is reported they did, but also whether what they did was right. Will justifies his return to killing by a desire to provide for his children; his hog farm is not prospering and his children will starve. They have killed before for money, he reminds Ned, but Ned comments, "We thought we did." Significantly, it is the recital of the (exaggerated) tale of the mutilation of the prostitute that sways Ned; no one who harms a woman deserves to live, because women, even whores, are necessary if men are to tame the wilderness. This is not a surprising response from Ned, who clings so hard to his wife and his farm, which, for a Black American in his time, represents a path to assimilation if not to salvation.

Not far into the friends' journey, Will begins to reflect seriously on his past, not formulaicly rehearsing his sins as he had done earlier for his children ("I seen the error of my ways . . . the sins of my youth") but thinking about the concrete effects of pulling a trigger. Close-ups of Ned and Will allow Will's almost deadened delivery to convey more power than his words, as he begins what will become a refrain of recollections on the brutal facts of death, memories of what happens when a bullet rips into a skull or a chest. Teeth fly out the back of the head, brains spill out. "He didn't do anything to deserve to get shot." Will in his redeemed self has abandoned whatever superiority he enjoyed as hero of a legend and is "just a fella now. . . . No different than anyone else—no more."

The memories of violent deaths, deaths that he himself caused, provide constant visual reminders of Will's own mortality: his trouble catching his hogs, his difficulties mounting his horse (he blames both failures on his earlier mistreatment of animals; his son judges with a shrug or a glance at his little sister that Pop's powers are failing). He can no longer sleep on the ground without discomfort and illness; he is slow and tired during most of the film. It is significant that Will, English Bob, and Little Bill are all of a "certain age," totally unlike themselves as figures in their legends. Heroes are not supposed to age or reflect on the morality of their actions. Legends not only inflate intentions and deeds and conflate versions of stories, they also stop time—they defeat aging and death itself.

The Kid's stories are such oral narratives, vivid and insistent. English Bob, another wandering gunslinger, not trusting public admiration to spread his legend, travels with his own personal chronicler, who takes "certain artistic liberty" with the facts, just as Bob has embellished his own history and has remolded his Cockney self into an aristocrat. Little Bill, by contrast, insists on the truth both about written accounts of Western history and about the human condition: All men are violent. If civilization is to continue in America, he reasons, it can do so only if men such as himself hold absolute power. The "six armed men" who once drove out Frank Miller are a permanent fixture in Big Whiskey, where Little Bill dispenses justice with complete abandon because he is within the law; he enforces morality by violence.

So "reality" in this version of the West is not just what is shaped and told about the past, or what is shaped and written, but also what the West itself reveals about human nature. Human nature is as violent and as lawless as nature itself. To romanticize stories about men's exploits is to invite a futile hope for a redeemer, just as the prostitutes wait and hope for a secular savior to appear.

Little Bill plays in a minor, distorted key what William Munny plays in a major one. He is Will's opposite-echo and his mirror-image. Where Little Bill bows to a certain knowledge about human nature that denies the spiritual power of the redeemer-myth, Will holds no such false ideas about himself as a savior, in either his past or his present roles. In the past, he says, he was drunk most of the time. In the present, he only needs money. One last try to catch his hogs to separate them is followed by a visit to his wife's grave, then a glance at her photograph, and immediate attention to cleaning himself and his gun. She would recognize the higher calling that leads him to kill again: He will feed their children. But this he does while knowing that he "ain't like that no more," hoping that this bounty killing can be accomplished without staining his innermost spiritual and precious self, the self saved by his wife's love.

On every level Eastwood satisfies the spectator's desire for engagement, puzzle, and a fear of death combined with a hope of resurrection—resurrection for the individual and reconstitution of the fragile social order. At the point of death, Will "sees" the Angel of Death and "sees" his wife—not only on the plane of spiritual reality, as Ned thinks, but at the level of phenomenon (physical reality), as her rotting corpse would appear if exhumed. The dying man's head is cradled by his beloved friend in the imagery of Mary holding the head of the dying Jesus. This presents the climax of the train of shifting postures toward death in the film.[12] Will confesses to Ned: "I seen the Angel of Death. . . . He's got snake eyes. . . . I'm scared of dyin'. I seen Claudia, too. Her face was all covered with worms. I'm scared. . . . Don't tell nobody. Don't tell my kids none of the things I done, hear me?" Death is "really" like young Davey's, with blood and thirst and abandonment; it is "really" the end (of the life we know) and should not be glamorized, as The Kid realizes when he actually kills a living, breathing human being. What is important to leave after you die is not "legends" or even facts about killing, but a heritage of love and trust—those virtues Claudia had stimulated in Will during her short life.

Little Bill attempts to quash the prostitutes' hopes for a savior and puncture the myth that might bring gunfighters and disruption back to his town. Ironically, when he carries his attempt to hold disorder at bay to its logical extreme by killing Ned, he activates the mighty redeemer myth—indeed, this calls all the forces of the Western from James Fenimore

Cooper to Zane Grey to John Ford to Howard Hawkes to Sam Peckinpah down on his microcosmic settlement. Ned has "died for what we done," as Will says, died *exactly* — not *symbolically*, as his wife had — for Will's sins. Ned's body is exposed in the public square, Christlike, with wounds and a sign. The William Munny who enters the saloon the second time, gun barrel first, is a Will reborn not just of whiskey and his own bloody past, but of Ned's sacrifice in the name of all that keeps human society from degenerating into a living embodiment of Death: love.

Ironically, it is impelled by *love* that Will is re-created as the quintessential hero of the myth even as he commits the unthinkable, killing even unarmed men in the name of a justice that transcends Little Bill's petty tyranny. The expression on the writer's face when Will enters the saloon expresses the shock of recognition both for him and for the audience; this is the real item, a living legend, a hero-savior who will cleanse the land of its hypocrites and torturers, those who "cut whores" and fail to give the honorable and loved dead a proper burial.

At the end of the film, director Eastwood closes the story frame by repeating the tableau of the golden horizon from the opening sequence and by terminating the "tale" of Will Munny with a brief written text. As the hack book *Duke of Death* (intentionally) garbled the truth about English Bob, and as words in the film often mask truths about persons or situations, the final words that scroll down our screen (despite their power to evoke mystery and moral outrage) are inadequate for understanding the visual drama that we have just seen and experienced.

The scrolled text reveals: The mother never understood why her "only daughter" married a "known thief and murderer, a man of notoriously vicious and intemperate disposition." Even an only daughter can leave home and marry for love; however, despite her goodness, and even though she doesn't "deserve" to die, nature will take her, merit or none. But as Will says to Little Bill, "Deserve's got nothin' to do with it." The mystery is not why the young woman had married Will, but how she managed to transform him and live with and through him after her death, even through his bitter return to a bloodshed that is depicted in the story as purgative and inevitable.

What remains after the scrolled text has disappeared from the screen is our confused reaction to the justice and reward meted out in this story world. Earlier versions of the Old West (even Sam Peckinpah's *The Wild Bunch*) were somehow more comforting, perhaps because so many of them nested so securely within the boundaries of the Western formula: corrupt gunmen, good sheriff or lone gunfighter, pure woman, satisfying conclusion. *Unforgiven's* ending allows multiple interpretations, readings that can range from disgust at its "gratuitous violence" to "violence appropriate to the context" to "complete rejection of violence." A troublesome note little-mentioned in commentaries on this film is its last reference: that Will Munny and his children "are said to have prospered in dry goods"—a complicated reference to further mythmaking, to Will's commitment to his children's welfare, and to the benevolent use of the reward money earned at such a horrible price. Are we to judge Will, to praise him, or to identify his redeemed, ravaged, and reclaimed life with our own pilgrimage toward healing and celebration?

Ambiguity—uncertainty about what this film means— remains long after the movie is finished, and so do its powerful *mises-en-scène*—the isolated cabin rimmed by distant mountains; the hotel, which represents the little that exists of family, food service, and human connection in this town; Little Bill's crooked house, physical symbol of his desire to create a civilization with his own hands, by his own (crooked) code; and the near-death sequence in the hideout cabin.

With Eastwood's technical expertise, he could have shown us a replica of the Old West. What he does is create a feel for the sordid daily reality of the old settlements. He accomplishes this, however, without sacrificing the deep truths about life. By constant close-ups and shifting camera angles (as in the final saloon scene), he reveals a palpable and insistent fear of death in men who, according to the myth, should know no fear. He shows not only through faces but by the physical positioning of the prostitutes (almost always on the stairs or looking out the window) a longing for purity, which transforms the face of the mutilated blonde prostitute—as she stares at the retreating form of her avenger, rain (or tears) streaming down her face—into the lovely face of a Madonna. Simultaneous versions of the "redeemer" theme are held in tension at the end: the redeemer as cleanser, like the rain, but also the redeemer as the wish-fulfillment of a passive and misled viewing public. The killing may be seen as driven by the whiskey Will consumes, by the driving force of the American myth of "justice," and/or by the opposition from heaven of equally evil killing and torture as performed in the name of "civilization." Any one-dimensional glorification of violence is undercut by all that has gone before in the film, even as the dramatic structure pushes the story to its violent conclusion.

Deep inside Will's stories and our own, Eastwood shows Will's and Ned's poignant longing to know the meaning of the proscriptions of Scripture ("Thou Shalt Not Kill") and a desire to believe in an afterlife that will remove uncertainties about moral behavior. This raises the question: Are our precious friendships part of a larger plan? This is a film of great spiritual richness and great physical beauty that dares to turn ideas about justice upside down; that asks again and again when, if ever, we need to kill; and that insists throughout that as flawed human beings, we *can* and *must* be redeemed by love.

QUESTIONS 1. Some critics have adopted this movie as a "feminist text." (Eastwood himself has referred to himself as a "feminist director.") Certainly the movie's treatment of women on the frontier departs from earlier representations of women as either mere prostitutes or models of civilized and virginal behavior. The prostitutes are portrayed as active entrepreneurs, for instance. How does Eastwood develop this idea? Does this neutralize or enhance their moral stature? Does he romanticize them or their profession?

2. What does the scene in the hideaway cabin, between Will Munny and the mutilated prostitute, add to the overall drama? How does the staging of this exchange affect our response to their dialogue? Discuss pastoral care in relation to this situation.

3. Among the oddities of the plot are Davey's attempt at restitution (when he brings the victim a pony) and the willingness of the victim to forgive him. Why does Eastwood back away from such a solution to the problem? What does the story gain when such an "ending" is frustrated?

4. Will Munny's wife is a powerful force in this drama, recalling the importance of the Quaker wife in *High Noon*. L. Gregory Jones hints that Will's wife's influence is lost over the course of the film. In *Unforgiven*, he writes,

> forgiveness is assumed to be impossible or, at most, ineffective. Habits of sin, and more specifically of violence, are inescapable; they cannot be unlearned. Violence is the inescapable reality that persistently tears at the fabric of people's lives until everyone is diminished, if not destroyed, by it.[13]

Is vengeance seen in this film as ultimately more powerful than forgiveness? Would you characterize this as a bleak, despairing film that glorifies or at best accepts violence as a solution to problems? What situations, characters, and messages in the movie might contradict this analysis?

Lone Star
John Sayles, 1996, 137 min.; R

In 1910, my grandfather took his sick wife and surviving children, my mother among them, and headed south for Paris, Texas. Plagued by collapsing cotton prices and the Paris fire of 1916, the little family returned north in 1918, but not before Grandpa had laid a network of corduroy roads, established schooling where none had ever been known, brought Midwestern-style Methodism to Bogota, and made lifelong friends with other wanderers.

We followed Grandpa some fifty years later, migrating to what was then perhaps Texas's least-inhabitable area—Houston. Each week, thousands surged into that steamy, inland, concrete paradise—like us, young and ambitious, eager to cross borders and defy old social codes. Unlike the white Protestant European culture that had fed the Midwest in the 1850s, this newer culture was white, black, and Mexican American, with its Native American past not gone and its religious obsessions up front. Money was easy; the oil and real estate boom propelled Houston's transients from obscurity to visibility and the city itself from cow town to international player in medicine, the arts, and business.

That was thirty years ago. Since then, Houston, like other Southwestern cities, has passed in and out of stardom. What remains is what has always been there beneath the monied surface: a pride in the frontier virtues of individualism, integrity, and independence that sustained peo-

ple like my grandfather against hostile weather and loneliness and an uneasy relationship with Texas's past as Mexican territory.

Lone Star is a deeply moral probing of those two poles of
Texas myth and memory—white conquest and Mexican presence. Added to this mix are the African American Texans. The
issues are serious: Who has control over education and history? What do we teach our children? When cultures live in
proximity, it is important that they hold common ideas about
what constitutes ethical behavior? How do and can minority
or marginalized ethnic groups acquire and hold economic
power? What happens to justice when two or more cultures
come together? Director Sayles' concern in this movie, like
that of John Ford and Clint Eastwood, is to understand the
myths that shape and sustain an America of continually shifting ethnic identities. He probes personal and national identity
through a number of compelling stories, one involving an
unsolved murder.

PLOT Two prospectors uncover a rusty sheriff's-star out on a
long-deserted local military firing range. The town's current sheriff, Sam Deeds, Jr., suspects that the badge and the
bleached bones uncovered nearby belong to his father's rival and
enemy, Charlie Wade, a corrupt law officer who exacted payoffs
from and murdered at will among the county's Mexican American population. Sam, thinking his father guilty of the murder,
sets about to expose the great Buddy Deeds for the fraud he
believes him to be: not a man of integrity, but a man whose legend is based on false assumptions of honesty and fair dealing.

Woven in with this massive investigation of cover-up is
Sam's own past. More than twenty years earlier, Buddy forced
Sam to give up the only woman he ever loved, a Mexican
American named Pilar. Buddy Deeds was "judge, jury, and
executioner" in private life. Buddy ruined his son's life, and
now his son sees a chance to get even.

This is a community at war—with history, with legend, with crime, and with cultural incompatibilities. The larger American experience is present in the form of the military base, whose soldiers are largely African American enlisted men and women and whose leader, Colonel Delmore Payne, is, like Sam Deeds, a former inhabitant of this border town. Delmore seethes with resentment against his father, Otis, who deserted the family when his son was eight years old. Otis now owns the only bar in town where African Americans are welcome.

Sam solves the crime. Pilar reenters Sam's life, as does her mother, a successful local businesswoman. Romance blooms. Some conflicts are resolved, and others, in the tradition of great narrative, are left open-ended.

REFLECTIONS *Lone Star* is about clashes of cultures—clashes fought not on the battlefields, but in the homes, in the schools, at the ballot box, and through storytelling. Of Texas's history, John Sayles has written this:

> Texas is unique among the United States in that it was once its own country. It was a republic formed in a controversial and bloody way. And its struggles didn't end with the Civil War. There is a kind of racial and ethnic war that has continued. That continuing conflict comes into the clearest focus around the border between Texas and Mexico. . . . A border is where you draw a line and say, "This is where I end and somebody else begins." In a metaphorical sense, it can be any of the symbols that we erect between one another—sex, class, race, age.[14]

Each historical image is a metaphor for something larger and more troubling. For instance, the Alamo represents the appropriation of history by the winners (those who settled in Texas and drove out the indigenous Native Americans and Mexicans) to shore up territorial conquests. "Freedom" for Texas meant joining the Confederacy to allow slavery to be extended to aid cotton growers (and increase profits). What was once the Native Americans' ancient hunting grounds quickly became enshrined in legend as sacred land for white settlers such as the ones portrayed in *The Searchers*.

The military subplot in the movie highlights another type of clash: military versus civilian, law and order versus vigilante justice, "us" versus "them." Colonel Payne, Sam Deeds's counterpart, resembles—more obviously than does Sheriff Sam—the hero of the Old West (or the knight of medieval legend). He adheres to a strict code of honor both on-base and off, believing that persons must rise through merit and maintain honor by total dedication to a set of rules. That code, he learns, must be broken when human beings and their needs and desires are involved: his son's desire to follow his own heart; his father's longing to reconcile with the son he had deserted forty years before; his own soldiers' needs for a carefully balanced regime of discipline and support.

Was Buddy Deeds a righteous man? His name hints at a double nature. "Buddy" indicates a chumminess that might overlook justice for the sake of self-interest or community popularity. "Deeds" implies that he is a man of action, direct and honorable, like the hero in Frank Capra's well-known film *Mr. Deeds Goes to Town* (who is straight-talking but also rather naive).[15] When *Lone Star* begins, Buddy does not exist other than as a creation of the needs of his friends and his son. He is all legend, and, as we learn, that legend is self-serving for the persons narrating his "story." He is indeed implicated both in a murder and in a massive cover-up.

But just as manufactured stories about American history—such as the legends surrounding the Alamo—can't retain their believability forever, so also the legends about Buddy Deeds can't erase the guilt of the storytellers. Part of the search for a criminal involves the search for the self. The self can never be found until the person discovers that the other whom he or she fears—regardless of the ways in which that other may be different—is actually a part of himself or herself—a mirror image, a half-brother or half-sister.

Here lies the heart of this complex and troubling movie. Integrity, as embodied in Buddy Deeds, includes adultery, payoffs, cruelty to his child, and desertion of his wife. His integrity also contains the reverse side of human actions: rescuing the widow and orphan; protecting the defenseless from beatings or random murders; and creating an atmosphere of justice and peace.

Good and evil are never completely divorced in this film. (The continuity of past and present and the inescapability of past actions is reinforced visually by Sayles' use of a seamless transition from present to past, panning without a cut.) In order to do good, Buddy Deeds must do some evil. He cannot allow his son, Sam, to marry Pilar, because she is Sam's half-sister. At the same time, he cannot admit to having had an adulterous affair with a Mexican American woman, because he lives in society where bigotry rules supreme. (So-called miscegenation seems to trump adultery in the list of wrongs in this town.) Buddy lost his son but protected what he may have regarded as the greater good: a community where African Americans and Mexican Americans can live and work without fear.

QUESTIONS 1. In all parts of the movie's story, "codes," whether written or understood, are examined. This includes what is known in the Christian Scriptures as the Ten Commandments. Does being a person of integrity require that you keep all the Commandments, or are there times when human suffering requires that you look at righteousness from another angle? What of reconciliation and mercy?

2. Director Sayles tackles subjects that other filmmakers ignore, dismiss with a screen smile, or trivialize—such as racism, not only against African Americans but also against Mexican Americans. How does Sayles deal with racism? What parts of racism has he chosen to dissect? What are the implications of his revelations about Mexican American immigrants, for instance? How is interracial romance handled? Do you find his portrayals satisfying?

3. How does Sayles handle American history? Do his characterizations (Texas of thirty years ago) and conflicts (the debate over school textbooks) close down or open up discussions about issues of our common history? How? Does Sayles make his own point of view clear, or does he give time and space to different perspectives? How and where?

As we struggle to bring about peace and act justly, the Kingdom world may break into this one through unexpected channels. Interference with earthly affairs by agents of the afterlife always has been a favorite movie ploy, from Stairway to Heaven *to* The Preacher's Wife —*by angels* (Michael; Wings of Desire); *ghosts* (High Plains Drifter, Ghost), *or even the devil* (The Witches of Eastwick, The Devil's Advocate). *We may be warmed or amused by such plot devices, but they rarely change us.*

In each of the films in this chapter, however, the hero or heroine is not given worldly or otherworldly power, but is quite unmistakably weak, defenseless, vulnerable, or impaired in some way. Some would characterize each of these distinct character types as a "fool" —a definition, for movie-discussion purposes, that we will explore more fully in this chapter. There are no sermons, and there is no interference from beyond the grave (except in Forrest Gump, *by the animators' craft); the fool often lives on the margins of society or has been rejected by society. "Despised and rejected," the fool draws out evil or goodness from other persons, who may be judged by their response to "the least of these who are members of my family" (Matthew 25:40).*

PURITY OF HEART

Forrest Gump
La Strada
Sling Blade

INTRODUCTION

> ## *"She died of goodness."*
> *Doctor, in* Breaking the Waves, *speaking of Bess, the heroine*

A recent star vehicle for Jim Carrey, *Liar Liar* (1997) casts the comedian in the role of a slick lawyer who is "wished" by his five-year-old son to be compelled to tell the truth for twenty-four hours. The result is total chaos in the workplace. The humor hinges on the disparity between what a person thinks and what he or she says and does—intentions filtered through social convention (never let anyone know what you really think) versus the mechanisms of professional success (use language to manipulate people and situations to your own advantage). That the Carrey figure is a lawyer is all the better.

Once transformed into a truth-teller, whom does Carrey resemble? Not any of us, with our carefully learned deceptions. He is like a fool or a child. The fool by this definition is an individual who acts simply, without guile—a person for whom there is no gap between *intention* and *action*. In Carrey's case, the comic device—to turn a master manipulator into someone who cannot do other than tell the truth—not only creates an occasion to showcase the talents of this elastic comedian (successor in shenanigans to Steve Martin, Jerry Lewis, and Danny Kaye), but it also allows the plot a happy ending.

Transformed by his son's heartfelt wish, the Carrey character may lose his place among the movers and shakers, but his rewards are enormous: a bond between himself and his son; greater self-knowledge; and a huge list of ways to live in the contemporary, success-driven world while retaining the fresh perspective of the truth-teller. *Liar Liar,* like *Jerry Maguire,* is a lighthearted version of the *Wall Street* theme: Money and success don't have to corrupt.

The narrative formula is unbeatable. An audience might cringe at a sermon on the screen but laugh at seeing its own hypocrisies acted out in vivid color. Even in a Hollywood blockbuster comedy, where the lines between honesty and deception are artificially drawn, self-discovery can seep in. It may be possible to retain integrity and still live in our modern world. Unfortunately for serious soul-searching, rewards are delivered rather easily, as though a change of heart can bring love, friendship, and self-respect but deliver no damage to the professional career. Real life doesn't always work this way; but, after all, this is a gently prodding comedy, not a savage satire.

REFLECTIONS Part of comedy's appeal is that it challenges pretense—someone slips on a banana peel, someone dignified is caught in public having a bad hair day or wearing last year's suit. Pulling the mighty down from their seats, the yearly "Feast of Fools" in medieval Europe took literally the majestic text from Luke 1:51*b*-52: "He has scattered the proud in the thoughts of their hearts. / He has brought down the powerful from their thrones, / and lifted up the lowly" (NRSV). For one day, the poor were elevated and the rich debased.[1]

Reversal is the key idea. Whatever century, whatever culture we live in, our lives are closely defined within certain restraints: the church, government, social class, racial identities, gender prejudices—or the insidious groupings within which we find ourselves trapped, neither secure nor brassy enough to live and love freely. Do we buy the right hair-care products or sport this year's fashions? Are we slim, young, and beautiful—or rich? Privately, we want to escape, to be able to make choices about friends and beliefs that are not determined by others. Publicly, we're cautious.

Here may lie the enormous appeal in literature and film of the figure of the fool, who embodies a reversal of imprisoning stereotypes. The "wise fool" lives in the kingdom of God in the present, with its radically different way of evaluating the world's hierarchies. Christ perfectly embodies this concept, for worldly pride and wealth mean nothing in the perspective of eternity.

The fool is one who is or has become pure of heart, one who, in the words from the Beatitudes, "will see God"

(Matthew 5:8). What does it mean to be pure of heart? Do we have to lose our power to reason, our *good sense,* to gain this mysterious purity?[2] Does reason cancel out goodness? Is this a matter of birth or of will?

In the New Testament, the blessing on the pure of heart is part of a larger vision of the kingdom of God—living simultaneously in two worlds, the time-bound and the transformed. The scriptures are rich with parables that illustrate the qualities of that life: loving one's God and neighbor, the neighbor imaged as the most unlikely candidate, a Samaritan (Luke 10:29-37); appearance, position, worldly power—none have worth beside the riches of the kingdom of God (Luke 12:22-34). In this new assessment of traditional values, "purity of heart" is not limited to the scrupulous observance of religious ritual, but rather includes cleanness of intent. Your thoughts and actions should be of one piece. There is an absence of calculation or manipulation in what Jesus' words proclaim—you must treat a person as a person, not as a pawn on your road to salvation.

To understand these tough passages seems a superhuman task; to live by them may seem beyond hope. Radical reversals lie by nature at the heart of stories, which often are motivated by a wish to capture a moment when the author was conscious of a loss of innocence *(Lord of the Flies; Stand By Me)* or caught a new vision of the world *(Crime and Punishment; Gandhi).* What Jesus preaches is not plot-bending *peripeteia* (a sudden change in circumstances), but life-changing *metanoia*—a turning of the person, getting a new spirit, as Psalm 51 (verse 10) pleads: "Create in me a clean heart, O God, / and put a new and right spirit within me" (NRSV).

We're a long way from *Liar Liar.* Or are we? The title of that movie is taken from a child's taunt: "Liar, liar, pants on fire!"—a variation of the essayist Montaigne's tongue-in-cheek reminder that "even the King in all his pomp and nobility is only sitting on his bottom." One of the many functions of comedy is to help us laugh at ourselves — to lift veils, take logs out of our eyes (Matthew 7:3-5), clean windows. Religious literature and fairy tales are full of such reminders that we need to take action to "see better." The fool, the one who is pure of heart, can clarify, can bring light to other people.

The child represents innocence — a lost time for each of us when it was a joy to open and shut a door, splash in a pool of muddy water, or wake up to sunbeams dancing across the wall. The elderly sometimes reclaim that innocence. In *A Passage to India*, for instance, the octogenarian played by Peggy Ashcroft is one of the few persons in her colonial group to intuit the goodness of the Indian Doctor Aziz (later unjustly accused of rape) and to respect his deeply held religious convictions. In *Wild Strawberries*, the protagonist Isak Borg discovers at age seventy-eight that it is not his medical achievements that shine, but his newly found childlike joy in friendship and love.

This is the fool as a "natural," as a person whose reason may be redirected (limited or impaired are not quite the right words) by age, birth, or illness. The revelations that cluster around the natural fool belong largely to us, the readers or spectators; it is the contrast between the simple, nondiscriminating honesty of this person and a duplicitous world that creates humor *(Forrest Gump)* or startling insights *(Sling Blade)*. This is the person who is "like a child," but before the poison of social or ethnic division seeps in — like Scout in *To Kill a Mockingbird*, who defuses a potentially murderous Klan assault on her father and his prisoner, a black man, when (recognizing voices and shoes) she calls her neighbors under their white sheets by their names. Or like the blind outcast Mr. Will (John Malkovich) in *Places in the Heart*, who scatters the Klansmen not by gunfire but by his ability to shame them by calling them by name.

Not one, but *two* such persons appear in the Dutch movie *Antonia's Line*. Loony Lips and Deedee are among the outcasts taken in by the majestic Antonia in the dark years after World War II. These sad persons, capable of joy or grief but not capable of free and reasoned choice, have been objects of the cruelty of a rich farmer and his son. Antonia's charity activates our judgment not only on those who reject, even torture, such loving (but "nonproductive") human beings, but also on her fellow townsfolk, who had betrayed to the Nazis a Jewish citizen and his protector.

Thus there is a third fool in *Antonia's Line*—Antonia. Although she professes no allegiance to the church (which, in her world, had remained silent during the Nazi persecutions), she is Kingdom-oriented as surely as if the Last Days were upon her. She is pure in heart in the other sense of Jesus' words in the Beatitudes—pure on the inside, but with a clear eye for the evil of the world, "wise as serpents, and innocent as doves" (Matthew 10:16*b*). Antonia stands in the tradition of the wise fool, the person who, as Paul writes, is a fool "for the sake of Christ" (1 Corinthians 4:10 NRSV). Erasmus, in honor of his dear friend Thomas More, wrote:

> Christ, in order to relive the folly of mankind, though Himself "the wisdom of the Father," was willing in some manner to be made a fool when He took upon Himself the nature of a man. . . . Nor did He wish to bring healing by any other means than by "the foolishness of the cross," and by weak and stupid apostles upon whom He carefully enjoined folly . . . while He incited them by the example of children, lilies, mustard-seed, and sparrows.[3]

This is a different kind of "purity of heart," then, a different kind of fool—one who *sees clearly* and *acts justly*.

The following films explore "purity of heart" in different ways. Forrest Gump is charming not only in his wide-eyed simplicity, but also because his creator repeatedly sets him in situations of stupidity or squalor where his innocence contrasts vividly with the active evil around him (racism, war). Gelsomina in *La Strada* is poor, female, and simple—three strikes against her. Yet she not only feels injustice, she reacts against it. The hero of *Sling Blade*, Karl, is a slow-talking natural whose simplicity affects everyone he meets. In both *La Strada* and *Sling Blade*, moral growth belongs not only to those within the story who encounter the pure in heart, but also to the "fools" themselves, who observe, feel, reflect, and act.

Is it possible to die "of goodness," as the saintly Bess does in *Breaking the Waves* (Lars von Trier, Denmark, 1996)? Gelsomina does. Karl in *Sling Blade* consciously sacrifices his freedom to protect the innocent woman and child who have sheltered him. The creators of *Forrest Gump* leave death to the old (Forrest's mother) and the "stained" (Jenny). In the tradition of the Hollywood happy ending, Forrest survives to entertain us another day.

Purity of heart, then, extends authenticity and integrity. The authentic life—oriented in relationship rather than alienation—is a life turned completely around, toward righteousness and mercy. "Purity of heart," the philosopher Kierkegaard wrote, means to "will one thing"—the Good—by willing to be holy as God is holy.[4] Purity of heart means being completely turned toward God—whether by birth (the natural fool) or choice (the wise fool), as we will see in the films examined in this chapter.

GOING TO THE MOVIES

Forrest Gump
Robert Zemeckis, 1994, 157 min.; PG-13

How well can an impaired person, a "fool," hold the fickle film audience? Very well indeed, as proved by a film that captivated audiences all over America. *Forrest Gump* follows the life and career of Forrest, who was born a bit "different"—with an IQ of 75, as the imperious superintendent of the local school system announces to Forrest's mother. The film manages to tap into almost every obsession dearly held by American conservatives and liberals alike—Horatio Alger and the American success story; the willing self-sacrifice of mothers; child abuse; drug use; romance; biracial friendship; Vietnam—the list goes on and on. This it does while displaying virtuosic genius with special effects, such as the falling feather in the opening credit sequence or the amazing Ping-Pong games.

PLOT Forrest Gump (Tom Hanks) tells his life story to all the folks who happen to sit down beside him at a bus stop. He was born somewhat less than brilliant and moreover had misshapen legs. However, his wonderful mother (Sally Fields) and his schoolfriend Jenny (Robin Wright) protect him from anyone who tries to hold him down. More amazingly, every time something of great historical significance occurs, Forrest just happens to be nearby, in the right place at the right time. He makes two great friends, Bubba (Mykelti Williamson) and Lieutenant Dan (Gary Sinise). Forrest makes lots of money. He falls in love, has a child, and becomes a responsible citizen.

REFLECTIONS No one could explain the enormous popularity of this movie, consistently ranked as a top film by polls of both men and women. This can't be happening! America has a long-running love affair with the dashing, intelligent heroes played by actors such as Denzel Washington and Harrison Ford. Forrest Gump, slow-talking and slow-witted, is the opposite of polymaths such as James Bond and the leader of the *Mission: Impossible* team, who could outwit any computer or human puzzle put in their paths. How could Americans love this character, we who have trouble accepting flaws—even minor ones—in our own children? Can the ambitious young professional whose aim is to emulate Tom Cruise,

Sharon Stone, or Wesley Snipes identify with a man whose mental age is nearer nine than twenty-nine?

Yes. Crafty director Robert Zemeckis recognizes that as dearly wed to action heroes and matinee idols as American audiences are, they love other things more: romantic love, sentimental death, and triumph over the odds. The movie's messages seem to be grandiose, yet simple: Anyone can make it in this grand country, even a simple person like Forrest; even a depressed, hyperactive amputee like Lieutenant Dan. Nothing will get in the way of motherlove—not even death! People who use drugs and protest a national war effort are wrong. The wages of sin is death, the movie suggests; thus Jenny, the object of Forrest's adoration, dies (presumably from AIDS complications).

The question is not what are the odds that a boy with multiple genetic limitations would run and Ping-Pong his way to fame (a question some viewers of this movie have asked), but rather, how could so many viewers think that the film represents only a testimony to the triumph of the human spirit or the rewards of hard work? It seems to me that its real genius lies in its mastery of technical manipulation, its exposure of social and religious hypocrisy (our own included), and its terrific humor.

This brings us to the question of reality and illusion in the movies. While manipulating screen images, director Zemeckis also manipulates our emotions. He shatters every illusion, including our fixation as a nation on "success" as the measure of a person's worth. (That is, Forrest was not appealing and lovable as himself, arguably, but rather because he outran the bullies, played college football, played great Ping-Pong, saved a life in wartime, and ran a successful business.)

If we fail to accept the film as a clever and committed comedy, if we think of it as "realistic," we are stuck with bumper-sticker sentiments: "No obstacle is too great if you work hard." "The lazy and the marginal will get what they deserve." "Drugs and premarital sex will kill you." What really works is the contrast between Forrest's innocence and the onscreen representations of the stupid and ill-willed, such as the school official, the bullies, the politicians who perpetuated an unjust war and resisted school desegregation, and self-important demagogues of either the left or the right. The movie doesn't deliver sermons in straights; it delivers them in spades.

What seems to be missing is a *clearly stated* judgment on the evils that the film presents. If the humor in the film arises from the "dissonance between Forrest's wide-eyed narration and Zemeckis's knowing direction . . . part of the joke is that Forrest doesn't get what's going on,"[5] the query then becomes: What can he know, given his limited intelligence? Or are we dealing only with a clever narrative manipulation by the filmmaker that divides the hero Forrest into two people: one, a man somehow smart enough to survive a war and become a millionaire; and the other, a man too "simple" to be aware of the implications of his life choices? Forrest is clearly meant to be "like a child"—perhaps a child trapped in a man's body, as in another Hanks hit film, *Big*. But as Robert Coles has written, even very young children are capable of moral intelligence—the ability to choose between good people and evil people, good acts and evil acts.[6]

Forrest Gump is a strange mix of the outrageous and the maudlin. Sadly, its brilliant use of the present narrator (in voice-over) to tell and comment on a past story is interrupted when Forrest stops being the comic narrator sitting on the park bench and becomes a "real-life action hero." Here the movie loses its humorous edge and slips into a pattern of easy reward ("I'm smart, Daddy") and punishment ("I did some things I shouldn't have done, Forrest") that puts its fool off his target and makes us wonder if the director also meant us to accept Forrest's earlier triumphs, such as his running career, as reality. I wish Forrest had stayed on his bus bench. Still, the big issues are all there for us to see and hear.

QUESTIONS 1. Director Zemeckis seems to be reaching for the daring message of *Breaking the Waves:* that total goodness in a flawed world may mean total sacrifice. *Forrest Gump* appears to have at its heart an ideal of moral purity and responsibility, an ideal that may be as completely realized by a fool as by a "wise" man. Does the movie succeed in portraying this ideal? How? How might it have been changed to make this point clearer?

2. Do you agree that Forrest "does not actively choose the good that he does"? Is it important that he knows what he is doing? Would the movie make its points clear even if Forrest did not act as an agent of change?

3. Is the movie tough enough, given the seriousness of the material introduced in the film (the Vietnam War, racial segregation, child abuse)? Do you agree that the plot breezes over disasters as though they only existed to show Forrest's invincibility and resourcefulness?

La Strada
Federico Fellini, Italy, 1954, 107 min.; Not Rated

Neither *Forrest Gump* nor *Rain Man,* neither *The Fisher King* nor *Being There* have duplicated the intensity of *La Strada* (The Street). Federico Fellini built *La Strada* around a young woman of limited intellect and life experience. He sets her in the world of the circus—the world of fantasy and foolishness that he loved.

PLOT Gelsomina (Giulietta Masina) is sold by her family to a traveling fairground wrestler, a strongman, Zampano

(Anthony Quinn). Gelsomina is ridiculed, ignored, and mistreated by the brutish performer, yet she finds pleasure in children's games, planting tomatoes, performing at the village spectacles, and playing music. Despite her pliable and long-suffering nature, she rebels against her ill treatment and runs away.

Gelsomina makes friends with the Fool, another traveling player who, although he is a professional, not a natural, fool (he makes his living by imitating the simplicity of persons such as Gelsomina), seems to be her kindred spirit. Through him, her world is imaginatively enriched; he speaks to her of hope and meaning, even though his "theology" can't explain either her suffering or his own death. Sadly, Zampano brutally beats the Fool, accidentally killing him. The Fool's death breaks Gelsomina's spirit. Burdened by Gelsomina's mourning and by his own guilt at causing the Fool's death, Zampano abandons Gelsomina. Years later, Zampano hears of her lonely death. Without her love, he has become drunk and friendless. Too late, he realizes how much he misses her.

REFLECTIONS This is a complex story, rich in religious imagery and mesmerizing in its visual beauty. Life is a journey of struggle, growth, and discovery. The metaphors that flesh out that journey are the stuff of myth, fairy tale, or religious story: the seed that blossoms forth; the sea that offers visual and spiritual refreshment; the contrast between innocence and guile, freedom and confinement, love and lust, trust and betrayal. The story unfolds like our own lives—sometimes routine, but more often full of the surprise and poetry that feed conflicting interpretations into the thirsty storehouse of memory.

Why use such strange characters: a simpleton, a strongman, and a professional fool? What—and whose—story is being told? Fellini, in responding to contemporary critics of the film (who disliked it as too mystical), stated quite specifically what he *intended* the film to be about. It was about "loneliness."[7] The mythic, he said, penetrates the everyday: A film can "incarnate in mythic figures" truths that a more strictly "realistic" film will fail to do.

The principal "mythic" element in *La Strada* is playtime. Work is play, and play is work—for Zampano, who travels around exhibiting his prodigious strength to crowds; for the Fool, who performs on a tightrope or a violin; and for Gelsomina, whose play ranges from beating a drum to clowning as a duck. For Gelsomina, play is the world of childhood, where she is most at home. Play is also the world of performance and fancy. Protected by the artifice of greasepaint and masks, actors are able to plunge spectators into fantastic imaginative journeys.

Fellini takes the image of the circus and stretches it in new directions. When Gelsomina is first taken from her home, she tells her sisters that she is going to be a great *artiste*. The phrase increases the sadness of her situation with Zampano. He never teaches her anything that reaches beyond his own needs—to wear a costume, beat a drum, announce his own act, and provide him with a free cook and mistress. What can she learn on her own? She mimics in ways that women traditionally have done: She tries to merge her identity with his, eating like he eats and imitating his voice.

Yet small things—a hat, a ragged coat—transform Gelsomina into a clown—a version of Charlie Chaplin's "Little Tramp." She wears the clown's face and, later, the clown's outsized costume; she walks the walk. Behind her costume, she is liberated; she exists in terms of play alone—that is, she exists for the spectators. She thirsts to expand this role—for instance, the comic routine she does with Zampano and her mastery of the trumpet. She is fascinated by the high wire and fed by the fellowship of the circus troupe.

But in what senses other than a role ("the fool as clown") does Gelsomina exist? Not as a woman, even though she has a sexual relationship with Zampano. Not as a friend to the strongman, who shows himself incapable of a relationship. Not as a neighbor, for if she remains with Zampano, she (like the tomato seeds she plants) will never be allowed to take root. The sequence at the wedding banquet reveals Gelsomina's isolation in all its pain. Contrasted with the affectionate couple who have married is the solitary young woman, whose "mate" is busily negotiating sex for a new suit of clothes; contrasted with the sumptuous wedding feast is Gelsomina's lonely meal of leftovers.

Gelsomina bonds best with children, who are not yet caught up in the schemes and artifices of the adult world. At the feast, she is taken from her lonely corner by the local children to meet the sick boy Oswaldo, isolated in a room high above the celebration. The encounter with Oswaldo marks a turning point in Gelsomina's life.[8] We never see Oswaldo; what we do see is Gelsomina looking closely at him, deeply moved. We expect Gelsomina to entertain him, draw him out of his loneliness, change the mood of the sick room, get the other children to adopt him as one of their own, and so forth. This would be a satisfying plot development at this point in the film, because we are longing for Gelsomina herself to be *recognized*—loved as a person in her own right, not as an instrument of Zampano's pleasure or occupation.

What we are given instead is a religiously charged scene. Oswaldo is in an upper room, gained by a long set of steps (always significant in films). If Gelsomina's description of him is accurate ("His head was THIS BIG"), then he is not only ill but was born suffering and misshapen, "despised and rejected"—a creature born into a world that cannot tolerate his deformity or understand why he lives. Oswaldo presents the extreme example of a problem only lightly suggested by Gelsomina's own deficits. The question is formed: What kind of deity allows the birth and suffering of little ones? Why are some persons born whole, intelligent, wealthy, and powerful, and so many others born broken, simple, poor, and desperate?

To introduce Oswaldo into the film pushes the purity of heart ideal to the heart of theological discussion. It may be charming to think of the "fools" of fiction or real life as blessed of God, but when their purity or simplicity brings them misery, then we have to ask if our admiration is one way that we refuse to face the problem of suffering.

Gelsomina may grow as a performer and musician, she may have moments of awakening about the world and her own self, but the more she grows, the greater is her capacity to suffer. She comes to know that her "difference" (her simplicity) has ill-equipped her to live independently and happily in this world. For some, even self-knowledge, even hard work, even purity of heart do not protect against suffering.

Gelsomina, despite the beauty of her unfolding spiritual life, travels a road that has no destination. She has no security and is always close to starvation. The circus she and Zampano join offers no more safety than the outside world of the street fairs. Even her friend the Fool cannot make her life right. All he can offer her is illusion (in his tightrope act he overcomes gravity) and a theology (everything in life has a purpose; otherwise God would have not made it).

Our final glimpses of Gelsomina in the film are not of her as a Charlie Chaplin-like comedienne or as a childlike sprite running about in nature, roles that would allow us to dismiss her as "charming." They are of her moaning, "The Fool is hurt," and lying in a sunny spot beside a partly destroyed wall. Even if her suffering and death somehow redeem the cruel Zampano, we must ask, Why must the good—the pure in heart—suffer?

QUESTIONS 1. Fellini never allows us to dismiss cruelty or injustice—excusing these by saying that Gelsomina's suffering is justified so that she can "represent" sweetness or comedy as foil to Zampano's unfeeling boorishness or as "spirit" against his brutality. How do you interpret the ending of the film?

2. Western society has always been conflicted in its treatment of those seen as limited in intelligence. How does *La Strada* open perspectives on the life and feelings of the poor or persons with disabilities?

Sling Blade
Billy Bob Thornton, 1996, 135 min.; R

Sling Blade, a "low-key drama about a simpleton murderer released from an Arkansas mental institution,"[9] opened in Chicago the day before Thanksgiving, 1996. It did so poorly in its first week that Miramax, its U.S. distributor, pulled it and limited its showing to the east and west coasts. It would be tempting to credit Miramax's marketing retooling of the film for its subsequent success, including its two Academy Award nominations (Best Actor for its star and Best Screenplay, which it won). The truth is that *Sling Blade* is not only well written, gorgeously filmed, and brilliantly acted, it also centers so squarely on the religiously charged theme of purity of heart that viewers may be forced to reconsider all that they ever thought about motivations, love, and the law.

PLOT Twenty-five years ago, Karl (Billy Bob Thornton), then twelve, killed his mother and her lover with a sling blade, a kind of scythe. He has served his time in a "nervous hospital" and is now released, supposedly cured. Karl makes his way back to his old hometown, where he gets a job fixing lawn mowers and is taken in by the town's other misfits: Linda, codependent on abusive boyfriend Doyle (Dwight Yoakum); Frank, a young boy; and Vaughan (John Ritter), Linda's homosexual boss.

REFLECTIONS In the summer of 1961, I lived and worked at a state mental hospital, one of only eleven orderlies (with a few doctors) assigned to care for 3,000 patients. From thirty-odd years' perspective, the setting—the lush green hills of Western Pennsylvania—seems oddly like the small southern town where released murderer Karl returns to begin a new life as a free man. My patients threw 300-pound oak benches, assaulted orderlies and one another when the moon was full, and chewed on their own flesh from time to time. Within two days of my arrival, I felt like I had slipped into an alternate time zone where all my accustomed defenses—my social dodges and my tidy values—were absolutely worthless. The experienced orderlies counseled me to keep pushing chlorpromazine at drug time and to stay out of the wards.

It was on the wards, however, that my own life, my routine trials and successes, fell into place as an elaborately constructed system of deceptions. My patients did not want to impress me; they had no interest in the abilities that brought me recognition in a small-college sorority-dominated world. They related to me as *myself*. I was a bit pressed in my heart to decide who that "self" was.

Sling Blade touched me deeply, right where I feel it keenest: in the dead of night, when I think with horror and amazement of the shortness of life and my own uphill struggle to live honestly and usefully within that brief time. I have lived in the South; I have lived in small towns. But when protagonist Karl gets off the bus that has brought him from the "nervous hospital" back to his old hometown, scene of his childhood suffering and his crime, I felt my urban self merge with his small-town past. I watched edgily to see what humiliations this odd man would suffer.

What unfolds on the screen is a remarkable modern telling of Matthew 25. The townspeople are judged (implicitly) by the way they treat Karl, a thirty-seven-year-old "fool." He is thrust like Rip Van Winkle from institutional protection into the world where he must make choices (even down to what to order off a menu). None of those choices is familiar, and many will not be good. How will Karl be treated: like a "re-tard" (as he is insensitively referred to in the film) or as a potential friend?

So far, the formula seems fairly familiar. The hero is a slow-talking, mentally impaired young man who must tell—and do—the truth. But while Forrest Gump is conveniently furnished with Hollywood's favorite resourceful and loving mom, Sally Field, and has a career winningly enhanced by the best technological tampering known to film, *Sling Blade* has a far different take on the world of the "fool."

Karl was born with no chances. He had no life with a family; once his "defects" were recognized, his mother and father made him sleep in a shed with a dirt floor, in the backyard. Much like Oswaldo, the imprisoned child in Fellini's *La Strada*, Karl is punished by his parents out of their own shame because he was born different. "They didn't want me up there in the house," Karl tells his new friend Frank.

The background details about the first twelve years of Karl's life emerge slowly, almost incidentally, through his peculiar, slow-talking storytelling style. His earliest story is delivered straight with no judgment or embellishment. There was a "little ol' shed my daddy built." He just sat in the shed, tinkering or just sitting, "starin' at the wall." He went to school briefly, but kids were "cruel." One particular boy was especially cruel. This is one of the people Karl killed.

Karl was a child with no life outside a dark shed, starved and (we find out later) beaten. Even the Bible teaching he received turns out to have been wrong, as he discovers when he learns to read the Bible himself. (Although we are not told this, we might guess that his mother told him that he was cursed by God.) When Jesus spoke of the care we must give little children, he surely had boys like Karl in mind: "And whoever welcomes a little child like this in my name welcomes me. But if anyone causes one of these little ones who believe in me to sin, it would be better for him to have a large millstone hung around his neck and to be drowned in the depths of the sea" (Matthew 18:5-6 NIV). The abuse Karl has suffered, some say, could lead to exactly the violent acts he commits.[10] Violence begets violence. But the "sin" (and Karl's returning memory of it) goes deeper than those murders or even the memory of the abuse he suffered. Nothing marked him with more reverence for life or more regret than the death of his little brother. This is the most shocking of the many revelations in the film. When he was "no more'n six or eight," Karl's father handed him a bloody towel and told him to throw it away. A small baby "no bigger'n a squirrel," still crying, was wrapped inside. Karl buried him in the woods.

In the film, the baby clearly is a stand-in for Karl, who also has been buried alive—first in the shed, then in the hospital. (In fact, when we first catch sight of the inside of the shed where Karl had lived for twelve years, we see a dark hollow in the dirt floor: What should be a child's nighttime refuge, his bed, was little better than a grave.) As Karl resurrects the memories of his past, he begins to confront them, turning them over and over from a new biblical perspective and making them part of his developing moral consciousness. In a sad recasting of the parable of the prodigal son (Luke 15:11-32), Karl confronts his father with the baby's death and his own abuse. His father continues to say that he has no son. However, Karl has acquired enough perspective on his own past that he can now judge those acts as morally wrong.

What could ever make such a world right, where children are tortured and killed? The film centers on the moral life — how it is discovered, how it is lived. Karl and his new friend Frank are like twins: Frank is twelve, the age of Karl when he committed the murders, and Karl, despite his chronological age, is hardly older than that. He is like a little child in his absence of guile and his pleasure in simple things such as French-fried "potaters" and friendship. This is the age when children stand at the edge of adulthood and must think and act for themselves, when they decide what paths they will take and how they will respond to evil people and situations.

Frank is essentially a good child: loving, faithful, nonjudgmental, intelligent, and hardworking. It is he who in the end provides the moral center of the film, for he is born loving but suffers a series of devastating blows: poverty, his father's suicide, steady physical and emotional abuse from a father-substitute. Frank could turn either way in response to Doyle's abuse of his mother and himself. He could survive it. Or he could run away or kill Doyle, or turn to a gang for kinship (Doyle threatens to separate him from his mother, Vaughan, and Karl). Karl foresees misery—moral death—for this child who so reminds him of himself and of the little brother who had died.

Freedom is an important issue to Karl. Initially, he fears it. The world is too puzzling—too vast. When he returns to the warden the first day and says, "I don't care nothin' about bein' a free man," he speaks from an understanding of freedom as safety and certainty. When he returns to the hospital after killing Doyle, however, Karl has willingly sacrificed a different freedom, one he found so sweet (freedom to be loved; freedom to make choices), to protect his new friend Frank from repeating his own sad history of abuse and murder.

The film does not advocate killing people, however. What

it highlights instead is the radically free nature of the human will, even in someone as simple as Karl. When he is given chances—given satisfying work, treated with respect, allowed to form bonds of friendship and trust, and allowed to confront the stories of the Bible without distortions—Karl develops a keenly moral sense of right and wrong. Ray Pride speaks—correctly, I believe—of "near-Biblical atonement."[11]

The supper at Vaughan's house is a defining moment in the film's unfolding story. It is a meal of outsiders—a single mother, a young boy, two persons both simple, and two gay men. Their "difference" is highlighted, not only by Vaughan's comment that "certain parts of my life I have to keep private," but also by the revelation that he "ain't allowed at the First Baptist Church." Vaughan's confession of love for his guests has a communion ring to it: "I just want all of you to know that I care about each and every person at this table." "All who are present" accept one another without fear and without reserve. There is no exclusion at this table.

And the outcasts protect one another as much as they can in their powerlessness. Just as abuse leads to abuse, love gives birth to love. The hospital warden takes Karl into his own home and arranges a job for him; "good ol' boys" Billy Cox and Scooter accept him; Frank shares his secret place and his dreams; Linda makes him biscuits in the middle of the night; Vaughan trusts him with Linda's life.

This is home, a Kingdom place, where love is as Karl tells Frank: "I care for you more'n anything they is. You and me made friends right off the bat. . . . It don't make no difference where I was t'be. We'll always be friends. Cain't nobody stop that." Karl hands Frank a legacy: a bookmark predicting his happiness; his Bible; and *A Christmas Carol*—Dickens's great story of redemption for the most unlikely of persons.

QUESTIONS 1. Karl stands in the tradition of *Taxi Driver* and the saints, and prophets, who want to "purify this rotten world, wash away all the filth." The tool of destruction he uses to murder his mother is shaped something like the scythe of Death in medieval iconography. What relation does Karl's baptism have to the larger message of the movie?

2. Late in the movie, Doyle delivers a speech to Linda and Frank that is almost identical to the one Vaughan had given, including words of love. Why do you believe that Vaughan is sincere and Doyle is not? Does the way this scene is filmed help you judge Doyle's character and actions?

3. Why does Linda keep taking Doyle back? What does her story say about the human need for connection?

4. How do you interpret Karl's killing of Doyle? Is this a kind of redemptive violence in which Karl rids this little community of a dangerous man, or is this the act of a psychopath who is repeating violent acts of twenty-five years earlier?

5. Is Doyle's death "justified"? Or has the filmmaker deliberately excluded him from the possibility of rehabilitation? How might this situation have been resolved without violence?[12]

Many of the films discussed in part 2 present worlds that are in various ways empty or broken. Their stories draw to an end in different ways: with a visual frame that provides a feeling of artistic completeness, even if we are not confident the characters have been redeemed (Cries and Whispers; Unforgiven); *with death, but a death that bears some ritual meaning* (Sling Blade; Diary of a Country Priest; La Strada); *or with a gesture or event of reconciliation* (Solaris; Contact; Places in the Heart). *If the power of healing has worked its magic within the movie story itself, as in Robert Duvall's* The Apostle *(1997), then a "happy ending"—some longed-for miracle—may belong as much to the spectators as to any of the characters on screen.*

Perhaps only Carl-Theodor Dreyer in the daring film Ordet *has ever shown a miracle on screen, although Lars von Trier made a brave try in 1996 with* Breaking the Waves. *But in a few movies, joy just won't be contained. These films pull out the feast and set the feet to tapping. Celebration—meal, sacrificial love, and rejoicing in the face of death—makes its bold appearance, and we are returned restfully and thankfully to that home toward which all our journeys have been directed.*

SCENE: 7 / TAKE: CELEBRATION

Babette's Feast
Daughters of the Dust
Ulee's Gold

INTRODUCTION

> *"I'm just giving you life,*
> *and you're giving me life."*
>
> *Josey Wales to Ten Bears, his warrior counterpart, in* The Outlaw Josey Wales

From time to time the old story "Stone Soup" makes its rounds. Tired soldiers, dragging home from a war they neither started nor wanted, dazed from witnessing the senseless butchery of other young boys like themselves, stop in a small village to ask for food. All doors are closed against them. "We don't even have food for ourselves, much less some to share," they hear again and again. So they sit down to make stone soup—the fairy-tale version of striking water from a rock (Numbers 20:11) or feeding the five thousand with a few loaves and fishes (Matthew 14:19-21; Mark 6:41-44). Entranced by the prospect of witnessing either magic or miracle in these dark, postwar days, the villagers creep around the young men, who are busily stirring a beautiful rock that's boiling away in a borrowed cooking pot over their open fire.

You know the rest: "Ah, wouldn't carrots add greatly to this delicious stew!" the soldiers muse as they stir and sing. Someone runs up with carrots that had been hidden under the floorboards of a small cottage. "And onions! and potatoes! and cabbage!" More bustling ensues around hayracks and under mattresses. By evening, it's a miracle indeed. What flavors—what nutritional value—the lone stone has acquired, for along with their hoarded foodstuffs, the villagers have brought *themselves*. Legend has it that everyone received at least one bowl of the piping-hot stone soup, and the bountiful feast was followed by dancing and singing in the town clearing that lasted until dawn. The outcast soldiers served as merry hosts.

There are darker versions of this story, where festival release follows more sinister gatherings in a clearing or a village square. In these old tales, some act of violence has occurred that requires restitution or atonement when the sun rises to expose the dead. Brother lifts hand against brother; a group chooses a scapegoat to heap its frustrations and outrage upon. The Bible serves up story after story, each reflecting some buried memory of the shedding of blood, whether in ritual sacrifice or passion or wartime: Cain against Abel; David against Uriah, the husband of Bathsheba; Moses against the

Egyptians; the Israelites against the men, women, and children who inconveniently lived on land they believed was theirs by God's decree. Such stories have an eerie, modern ring through our perspective on the American Civil War, the My Lai massacre in Vietnam in 1968, or the mutual slaughter of Hutus and Tutsis in Rwanda only a few years ago (nearly one million people killed since 1994).

The greatest narrative representations of celebration take into account this dark side of life—both death, which is inevitable, and death-dealing human behavior, which is not. The power of celebration, dancing, singing, or feasting (or all these) even in the face of death, arises from creation itself— creating life out of the void. We gather to celebrate not honors or wealth, but the blessings of creation, where each person is *acknowledged* as loved and precious. Through sharing food, even gathering in thankfulness that "lo, the winter is past," we form the bonds that enable us to face violence and death. "Sacramental celebrations connect us with the memory of the past ... and hope for the future" and thus are both *conserving* and *renewing* rituals.[1] Such festivity connects the celebrants with the Creator who is the source of both life and love; evil must be recognized and confronted and the goodness of life affirmed.

REFLECTIONS The films that form the larger part of this chapter reflect exactly this complex intertwining of suffering—the pull of death—and celebration—the yank of life that cries, "Let's dance!" and tangos—or boogies and strips, as in *The Full Monty*—in the face of tragedy and loss. It may be significant that two of the three films in this chapter, *Daughters of the Dust* and *Babette's Feast*, feature women in central roles, and the third, *Ulee's Gold*, places a man in a maternal role. Such a division may not be so much by gender as by social and ritual role; however, men can nurture and shelter as well as women, as my husband and his father and his two sons have proved to me over many years.

What may be more important is to sever religious celebration, the life of prayer and faith and the Eucharist itself, from suffering and sacrifice if those latter demean life or seem to require a lifetime of self-laceration. Such devotion is not unknown in the history of Christianity (or other religions), but perhaps Eucharist embodies something closer to the spirit of "Stone Soup" or the miracles of loaves and fishes: that self-giving generates hospitality; that peace-offerings shock, but beget openness; that those who have been healed may heal others. The three movies we will explore suggest that feasting, singing, and dancing arise when persons leave their fearful shelters and enter into relation with their neighbors and with this good earth. The sacred is to be found in everyday life, where men and women face injustice or death but choose life over death—choose to practice peace and to open their hearts and homes to the world.

Before we look at these films, I want to recommend to you several others that recognize such intricate bonds among all people. The first is Ingmar Bergman's *Wild Strawberries* (1957). An honored yet embittered man of medicine, Isak Borg, is led out of self-imposed isolation into joyous connection with his estranged family, three random teenagers, various persons out of his past, and, by extension, the whole world. I would be tempted to call this "spiritual rebirth," were it not for the movie title's merry reminder of the sweetness and fragrance of wild berries—the natural fruits of the earth, God's burst of springtime charity for a weary world.

The second film is *Antonia's Line* (1995), which I have referred to in other chapters. This film honors hospitality toward the wounded and the weak, and it invites us, the spectators, to eat and dance in the face of death, as Antonia does when she feels she is about to die.

My third recommendation is *The Outlaw Josey Wales* (1976), a movie that shows a firm understanding not only of the inescapability of violence and death, particularly in frontier

American society, but also of the temptation to perpetuate the violence by further acts of bloodshed. Josey Wales's wife and son are murdered, and his farm is burned by raiders; he sets out to exact vengeance not only on the group from which the raiders came, but on the whole Union army as well. Quite unexpectedly, however, Josey acquires a new family: a wounded and orphaned young boy, whom he nurses and mothers; a castoff old chief; an abused Native American woman; two refugee women, one aged, the other simple; and two half-dead Mexican Americans.

Two moments in this film crystallize its meditation on life and death: first, a dance and feast that Josey's ragtag family hold in the clearing of their new home, an abandoned homestead; and second, the confrontation between Josey and Ten Bears, the warrior chief who is his rival and counterpart. Why should either man continue endless, mutually destructive battles? Why not choose life over death? This is a bold move, both inside *this* movie's story (Josey is merely one armed man against hundreds) and inside movie storytelling itself. To die in a burst of gunfire is what we're used to; it can provide a tidy solution to troublesome problems that any film might raise (such as land-theft and the murder or removal of the land's age-old occupants). To refuse to shed blood and to explore how all persons might learn to live together is far braver and far more difficult, as *Josey Wales* and other films in this chapter show.

One final movie illustrates the radical, communal, and essentially religious nature of celebration. In the concluding sequence of *Places in the Heart,* the camera slowly pans through the congregation of a small southern church. Suddenly, the viewer becomes aware that black and white, pure and vicious, blind, lame, and sorrowing, live and dead are all seated together. They are all taking communion, passing the peace and breaking the bread of life. How powerfully that scene contrasts with my memory of a sad day back in 1965, when I overheard a member of my local church protest the next Sunday's Communion exchange with a Chicago church. This long-time pillar of the church insisted that she would "never take Communion from a black hand." Of all the hard words I heard during that turbulent decade, this was the saddest. For Communion, like Passover, represents the greatest celebration of all: that we are all part of the body of God, who rescues and saves us.

Here we return to the story we began with, "Stone Soup," which belongs to a layer of folk insights. It may be through sharing these insights that we are healed and can begin the Kingdom life. In "Magic and Meal," theologian John Dominic Crossan suggests that Jesus charges those whom he has healed to go into the world to heal others, to share food in "commensuality" that recognizes the "interconnected complex of mutuality and reciprocity" that exists among people when they eat and celebrate together.[2] The feast is a sign that God is still alive in the world, ready to celebrate with all who are willing to break bread and form a new household of faith and festivity. In the breaking of bread we share God's body; in our dances, play, and song we celebrate life's goodness.[3]

GOING TO THE MOVIES

Babette's Feast
Gabriel Axel, Denmark, 1987, 102 min.; G

In *Babette's Feast* (and *Daughters of the Dust*), eating expresses spiritual healing and refreshment and becomes the visible presence of love within the household. (The title *Ulee's Gold* conveys this same message. The gold in the movie is literally the honey produced by Ulee's bees, but metaphorically it is the true "goal" of Ulee's life's journey—to leave his self-imposed isolation and move out into communion with the world.

PLOT Two beautiful young women while away their youth in a small town in nineteenth-century Denmark, church servants to their preacher father and his stern congregation. Each is offered a chance to escape: Philippa to Paris, where she might become a great opera singer, and Martina as the wife of a young cavalry officer, Count Lowenhielm, who visits her village. The young women's father doesn't exactly squelch these plans, but his influence with his daughters is strong, and they turn away the offers.

Some decades later, the sisters find a soaked and starving Babette on their doorstep, a refugee from wartime Paris (1871). Although the sisters' income is tiny, with Babette managing their household, the dried loaves and fishes (in this film, particularly *unappetizing*-looking fishes) are turned into an abundance of provisions. Babette drives hard bargains at the local shops.

There's more. Babette, who wins 10,000 francs in the French lottery, asks to prepare a real French meal for the sisters and their squabbling congregation. Now follows the amazing transformation of dark interiors and dark spirits into a festival banquet hall of warmth and color, as Babette turns out a meal literally for royalty—identical to ones she had served while she was head chef at the Café Anglais, the most exclusive restaurant in pre-war Paris.

REFLECTIONS In the Dutch Reformed Church, the Communion table is placed in the front of the church. In former times, communicants actually sat around a table for Communion, visibly linking meal and miracle. The congregation in *Babette's Feast* is Danish, not Dutch, though its heritage is kin, sometimes veering away from a reverence for the fullness of life's pleasures toward the stern and iconoclastic side of Protestantism. But the connection between Communion and common table remains.

In the house churches of the early Christians, the congregation assembled at the end of the day for a common meal. If we are to take the mission and miracle of Christ seriously, Paul wrote, all are equal at the Lord's Table. As Robert Jewett has written, "the love-feast system in Corinth welcomed persons whom the society held to be shameful in the sense of lacking honor or social prestige."[4] He quotes: " 'God chose what is low and despised in the world . . . to reduce to nothing the things that are, so that no one might boast in the presence of God' (1 Corinthians 1:26-29)." Paul's letter to the Corinthians hints that the wealthy arrived first and took the best food, while the poor and slaves ate the remainder—a violation of the spirit of the love feast. In John, in fact, the Last Supper is linked with foot washing.

It is this exchange in Corinthians—an echo of the lovely song "Magnificat" that centers Luke's account of Jesus' birth—which animates Babette's table. The food and wine she presents is the fruit of the earth and the sea, available to high and low. The contrast between what the congregation members expect (their usual ale fish and dry bread) and the extraordinary delicacy and richness of the dishes is hysterical. But we don't watch to make fun of the asceticism of the old pastor's dwindling congregation, with their crabby grudges and myopic visions. We experience illumination with them—and with the sad and cynical Count Lowenhielm, who by chance is included in the dinner party. This is bounty made possible by a miraculous event: not Babette's money, but her sacrifice. She has spent all her lottery winnings to bring joy to the community who sheltered her.

So all these elements combine in one meal: sacrifice (Babette's willing one), inclusion of the shamed (the old poor, but also the old rich), and confession (old grudges are released, old sins confessed and forgiven). Confession, often part of communion, is stimulated by the generosity of the meal. The history of your existence must be laid bare so that you may be lifted up.[5] But the drama does not end with the colors of the feast, set in low light against bright faces. After the meal, the communicants rush out into the night to join hands around the village well—dancing and singing to the beauty of the night and the loveliness of all created beings.

QUESTIONS The question of sacrifice arises repeatedly in this film. The sisters each give up a chance to live in the outside world, and Babette spends the money that would return her to Paris to prepare the magnificent feast.

1. How are the sisters' choices represented? What factors contribute to the refusal of each to take up life outside her village? In what ways does the film suggest that they are happy with their choice of the celibate life? In what ways does it suggest that they regret their losses?

2. What is the significance of Babette's profession? How might the film be interpreted differently if, instead of being a famous chef, she were simply a widow who has the ability to prepare magical meals?

3. Babette has been called a "Christ figure," that is, a person who willingly sacrifices her life and/or substance for others. Do you see Babette's gift as sacrifice? If so, might she have spent all her money in some other way—perhaps to provide long-term relief for the old parishioners or for others in this isolated village? How else might Babette have responded when she won the lottery?

4. Count Lowenhielm recounts the story of a famous French general who said that the only person for whom he would lay down his life was the chef of the Café Anglais, that is, for Babette. What significance does this tale have in *Babette's Feast*?

Daughters of the Dust
Julie Dash, 1992, 114 min.; Not Rated

Daughters of the Dust is one of the treasures of American cinema. Julie Dash, who conceived, wrote, directed, and coproduced it (with the help of ace cinematographer Arthur Jafa), struggled ten years to gather enough funds to make this film, and even then some of the actors had to go without payment. This is history—and a group of stories—that has been too little told: the stories of African Americans (most of them female), Americans who fought like all of our ancestors to reconcile their attachment to the old traditions with their hopes and dreams for a better future. In the case of African Americans, however, those traditions, those memories, have come through the fires of kidnapping, the splintering of families, and slavery.

PLOT Most of the members of Nana Peazant's family, the Sea Island Gullahs, are packing up to leave their lovely haven off the coast of South Carolina for the American mainland.[6] Nana (Cora Lee Day) implores them not to forget the ways of their ancestors, who suffered the murderous crossing from Africa and worked the land to survive. Others are less enthusiastic about the old ways, such as Cousin Haagar, who craves the modern life of progress, and Cousin Viola, who raves about the joys of mainland life and (Western) Jesus and can't wait to get back to "civilization." She is accompanied by her boyfriend, Mr. Snead, who has come along to photograph the grand family gathering.

Eli Peazant, another one of Nana's great-grandchildren, has other things on his mind. His wife Eula has been raped, and he is tortured by the fear that the child she awaits may not be his. The unborn child herself is undaunted by this squabbling; not only is hers the voice that narrates the story, she flits in and out of the frame, visible only to a few (actually, visible only to us, the spectators, and to a startled Mr. Snead).

Despite such troubles, this is an old-fashioned family reunion, complete with arguments, confessions, and great food. Even Yellow Mary, another Peazant cousin, and her girlfriend show up, welcomed by Eula and Nana and scorned by most of the other women. The conflicts between the old religion (Nana's) and the new (Christianity) are put to rest when Nana administers communion to her household, using both a Bible and a "Hand" (from the spirit world).

The boat sets off for the coast, leaving behind some people we thought would be enthusiastic to leave this old culture. We shudder for those who do leave; this is 1902, and they are heading for the big American cities — no Utopia, as history has revealed.

REFLECTIONS The dark part of the movie's *fabula*, its history, is revealed slowly during the film. The ancestors of the islanders had come to America in chains, many of them drowning en masse rather than living as slaves (though the legends have it that the captives walked right back to Africa on top of the water). The survivors of the slave ships worked the vats of poisonous indigo to provide color for the clothes of the privileged.

Notably, anger is not the dominant mood of the film. Reflection and love are, and celebration is. The movie is as concerned with conveying the colors and textures and feel of everyday life on the island as it is with advancing its central narratives, which are stories of conflict and healing. We see brightly patterned quilts, ingenious hair-braiding, native crafts, and wall designs — beautiful for their own sakes. This is a lush but not an "exotic" island, for its colors and richness are its natural dress, and its location is the home of the people who tell the tales.

How does celebration mix with redemption in this film?

Although the surface story is about leaving home, the individual tales that weave in and out of the movie create a larger fabric, one that wraps the hearer in a cloak of memory and tradition. It asks the same questions raised in many of the movies we've examined: Where is a person's true home? How can that be found?

The narrative of *Daughters of the Dust* combines linear, episodic, and responsive ways of telling stories, which creates excitement as events and chronologies overlap. Eli's story is *linear*—there's a sexual secret. He wants to find out who raped his wife. This theme is never dropped. Along the way, however, we uncover other stories, other *episodes*, such as the story of Nana Peazant and her husband, the different versions of the Gullahs' arrival from Africa, the story of Viola's conversion, the origin of Yellow Mary's sadness, and the romance of Iona (who cannot be "owned" by her mama) and St. Julien Lastchild. Throughout the movie we pick up a theme or hear a story, perhaps as when Mr. Snead attempts to interview an older man, or the Muslim islanders *respond* to the stories they hear. The tight unity of time (under twenty-four hours) is deceptive; this is a film that exits in many times, past, present, and future, and in many generations.[7]

Eli's story is the easiest to follow: It's like those we know from Hollywood movies, where the kidnapping or violation of a woman motivates so many plots. Eli's pain over his wife's rape has nearly destroyed his mind. He craves revenge on the man who violated her; only bloodshed will satisfy him. Further, he feels isolated from his roots. When Eli smashes the family's bottle tree (a talisman to ward off evil spirits), his is an age-old protest against a deity who, he feels, does not or cannot shield us from suffering and evil such as slavery or death or violation. His is an anger of impotence—he has no place in the developing world and no refuge in this one.

If this film were a Western or a thriller, it would be consumed with pursuit and punishment of the rapist. But this movie has other concerns, brought to the surface when the "lost" cousin, Yellow Mary, comes home to see Nana. Unlike the women who live on the island, Yellow Mary enjoys a life of freedom. She is well-dressed and travels at her leisure. She smokes, and she speaks her mind. She is not burdened with children.

Hatred for this "ruined" sister bristles among the women. It is Eula, insistent and fearful, who speaks to the gathering and connects the women's hatred with their shame over their own origins.

> Deep inside we believe that even God can't heal the wounds of our past or protect us from the world that put shackles on our feet. . . . We couldn't think of ourselves as pure women, knowing how our mothers were ruined. And maybe we think we don't deserve better, but we've got to change our way of thinking. We all good women. If you love yourself, then love Yellow Mary, because she's a part of you.[8]

Eula's plea brings all the story elements together. What lies behind the family's squabbling over territory and traditions is this legacy of shame—a feeling that just as the indigo from the vats penetrated workers' skin and couldn't be washed away, so the stain of slavery (and for women, the disgrace of being used sexually by slaveowners) has seeped into their spirits. Yellow Mary's humiliation includes having to suckle the children of her employer, even after her own baby has died.

Eula carries the shame of rape on her own body, and yet she doesn't consider it a burden. She is, she insists, still the wife of her husband and the member of a proud family: "We carry too many scars from the past. Our past owns us. . . . Let's live our lives without living in the fold of old wounds." The film offers a number of alternatives to living in the past, but one of the most beautiful occurs when St. Julien

Lastchild, the last of the island's indigenous peoples, sweeps in on a white horse, whisking his sweetheart Iona away from her grasping mother. We cheer this unexpected intrusion of heroic storytelling that rejoices in romantic love and free choice.[9]

This is a movie that celebrates life and locates home in the heart of the other person. As Patricia Mellencamp has written, " 'coming home' is recognizing oneself in others."[10] The "other" is no alien, no exotic, but one's own self, precious in God's life — not just an African American woman, or a woman, but all persons. As Karl Childers says in *Sling Blade* to young Frank, in whom he has recognized his innocent childhood self, "It don't make no difference where I was t'be. We'll always be friends. Cain't nobody stop that." That place is indeed home, a Kingdom space.

QUESTIONS 1. One of the questions that drives *Daughters of the Dust* is whether a person, or a group, can find freedom and redemption "within oppression."[11] In what ways does the film explore this question?

2. In what ways is the movie "about love and respect rather than fear and anger"?[12]

3. One of the many tragedies of slave culture was the difficulty of holding families together and the impossibility of passing along the old stories from which to draw strength. Describe the modes of storytelling used and the styles of family relationship celebrated in the film.

4. What might be some of the reasons Julie Dash has included among the islanders the Muslims, the Baptists, and St. Julien Lastchild?

Ulee's Gold
Victor Nunez, 1997, 113 min.; R

This is a remarkable film, notable not so much for the sustained dignity of Peter Fonda's portrayal of Ulysses Jackson, but for its insistence that all of life is infused with meaning. This film often speaks silently yet eloquently of home, authenticity, alienation, vocation, integrity, purity of heart, and healing. Ulee and his family are not heroes in the usual sense but are ordinary people who happen to live in the Florida panhandle and have been served up a large share of disorientation, deception, bad choices, and personal suffering. *Ulee's Gold* is no melodrama, but a beautifully crafted story of redemption and celebration.

PLOT Ulee Jackson has survived the Vietnam War, where every other person in his unit was killed. His beloved wife, Penelope, has died, and his son Jimmy is in prison for bank robbery. Ulee may not survive his last challenge: to leave the safety of his beehives and reenter the world from which he has so successfully and completely separated himself.

Ulee's son needs him. His granddaughters, Casey and Penny, who live with him, need him. His daughter-in-law Helen, dying from a drug overdose, needs him. Two thugs need him, or rather they need their share of the bank loot that Ulee's son has hidden; the thugs will kidnap and kill the girls to get what they want. The honey market also needs Ulee to fill its orders. "Trouble comes, and Ulee has to dismiss his own sorrows."[13]

REFLECTIONS This is a film about redemption. The hero, Ulysses (Ulee), reluctantly travels to see his son Jimmy in prison, a trip that turns into a massive, life-transforming journey for him and Jimmy, and for all the persons whose lives touch theirs. Along the way, the meaning of the title *Ulee's Gold* shifts from "Ulee's cash crop" to "Ulee's most precious treasure"—treasure as defined not by $100,000 buried in a swamp, but rather treasure that moths won't consume and thieves can't steal (Matthew 6:19).

Ulee's fractured household survives imprisonment, drug-induced delirium, full-scale teen rebellion, kidnapping, and a near-fatal knifing. As spectators who become deeply involved with the tragedies inside this fragile family, we expect a savior to rescue these innocents. Who will it be: an outsider—the sheriff? or an insider—Grandfather Ulee, sole survivor (both tricky and lucky) of his Vietnam unit? No savior breaks in, even though in terms of plot devices there are many chances for Ulee to "save" his family.

This is not a story governed by clichés, however, but by life. Our plot expectations are constantly frustrated. We learn Ulee is strong; we see him pin a young robber behind a door. Ulee was a killer in Nam; this could be the source of both his great physical strength and his anguish and isolation. Several times he has the chance to abort the robbers' plans. He could turn them in for extortion early or have them picked up. (He toys with telling the sheriff; we are told this not in words, but rather when the camera cuts to a shot of the sheriff, Ulee's old friend, as seen from Ulee's point of view.) At another point, the robbers are fixated on the loot; Ulee could stun them or kill them. "Kill them," his son pleads, but this isn't even an option for Ulee.

The underlying and untold story is Ulee's experience in Vietnam. We are given hints that this war completely ran his life off the rails. All he has now is the "vocation" of beekeeping—meaningless to him—inherited from nameless ancestors. (It is curious that nothing is revealed of Ulee's father or his heritage, other than this.) Penny, Ulee's youngest granddaughter, picks up a photograph of Ulee's Vietnam unit. Here, as so often in movies, a photo shows compressed history and feelings. Penny looks intently, then asks, "They're all dead?"

"That's right."

"Had they been bad . . . did they deserve to die?"

"No, no, Penny, they did *not.*"

"Why, then?"

"Those were good guys. . . . Your grandpa was tricky, lucky . . . that's why I made it out."[14]

Penny reflects: "When I hear about sad things it makes me go all quiet inside." This exchange captures the spirit in which the film has been made: Ulee's attachment to his unit; their deaths, undeserved; the injustice of war that would take young men from their families and send them to unprotected places; Penny's sensitivity to the sorrow and the waste of those deaths; Penny's empathy with her grandfather.

Like the young Frank in *Sling Blade*, Penny is not played for cuteness and cheap sentiment. Her questions arise from a child's innate curiosity about and theological sensitivity to the meaning of life. She is a wounded child, but (again frustrating movie clichés) she does not cut her body or harm others or run away. Once, early in the film, she does bolt out of the house, but it is to boldly seek a neighbor's help. (Her grandfather had scolded her: "We don't ask outsiders for help"—emphasizing the family's isolation. Ironically, the only concession to story convention I noticed was that the friendship initiated by Penny's action leads to a genuine rescue when Connie, the neighbor, comes to check on them and finds the girls and their mother tied up.) Penny responds to and expresses her sorrow through her art, her drawings, much as Victor Nunez, the creator of this beautiful film, has done.

Redemption in this movie comes unexpectedly, through loving the ones who love you. This is no sentimental love. This love firmly confronts death, responsibility, chance, and sorrow early in the film and explores its power in every corner.

Ulee's Gold ends in giggles in the kitchen: Helen, the former drug abuser brought back to life by Ulee's careful nursing, is making Christmas cookies with her daughters. The healing of

Helen, the rebellious Casey, and Penny has been remarkable. The camera moves in from the side to focus on a flour-covered Penny. She shows Grandpa a star—the star of Bethlehem.

Festivity and worship, mission and meal are united as Ulee breaks into his first smile. It mirrors the smiles we have seen earlier on Jimmy's face, when his wife and daughters and Ulee visit him in prison; they all laugh around a picnic table inside the correctional institution, planning for his release and return home. Father and son talk in odd shot/countershot, Ulee facing one way, Jimmy another. Will there be new life? Ulee's "gold" is the honey he sells, nature's purest food; his journey has been to care for his wounded family and to find that their care and love is both the trip and the goal.

QUESTIONS 1. "Jesus' invocation of the kingdom of God [is envisioned] not as an apocalyptic event in the imminent future but as a mode of life in the immediate present" (*The Historical Jesus*, 304). In what ways are these words lived out in *Ulee's Gold*?

2. In this chapter I have suggested that eating and healing belong together. In what ways is this borne out in *Ulee's Gold*? How does it come about in *Daughters of the Dust*? in *Babette's Feast*? In what ways do the films suggest that the healing might endure? Are you convinced? Why or why not?

3. Victor Nunez, director of *Ulee's Gold*, not only directs but also does most of the camera work in his films. Sometimes the camera is hand-held. Sometimes the focus remains on a person's body part, while the dialogue continues. Your mind reconstructs the entire scene. (One example is the opening, where we see Casey's legs and short skirt, arms, etc., but not her face. We create a picture of her from the parts and from the music.) How

does this unusual style shape the way you react to the film's story and characters?

4. How are the story's healings—Ulee's, Helen's, and Casey's—related to the discussion Penny has with Ulee about Vietnam? How are her questions answered within the film itself?

Part Three: HEALING

HEALING: A FILM DIARY

The English Patient

INTRODUCTION

"I found a plum in the orchard. We have an orchard."

Nurse Hana, to her dying patient

In 1997, *The English Patient* won Best Picture and eight other Academy Awards—a Cinderella triumph, considering that independent film studio Miramax picked the project up after a major Hollywood studio had dropped it as a potential loser. Why has this film been such a stunning financial and critical success? Miramax is a shrewd marketer of its movies, but that would not explain the broad appeal of the film or its garnering of artistic prizes. Why does the film stir such passionate response?

The English Patient is a film of remarkable visual power: a "stunning, seductive movie . . . resplendent, exotic, deeply and inexplicably stirring."[1] The richly poetic language of the novel from which the film is loosely adapted has been transmuted into poetry of the image—mythically charged signs; textured surfaces; iconographically rich compositions; weeping or smiling faces.[2] Like the archaeologist Count László Almásy, its stoic hero, the film speaks many languages: those of romance, war, epic, tragedy, theology, ethics.

The English Patient's carefully nuanced themes embrace our deepest concerns: the alienation of persons from whole and holy lives; the desecration of God's good earth; the activities of healing; and the consummation of the religious vision in the finished, new creation in God. The patient's memories, once barriers to protect his invincibility, become instruments of his healing and his salvation. The serenity of his face as he meets his death—a serenity enabled by the abiding care gifted him by his nurse and his tiny household—parallels the painful emergence of the earth from mud and war into a renewed cycle of growth, moving from brokenness toward new life.

Yet this is not a film without pain. Its surface is gorgeous, but beneath the layers of beautiful surface lie troubling ethical questions about private and public morality, questions about accountability. One way to interpret the movie is to see it as a battle between two views of human nature: that which cherishes memory and hope, and that which views human beings as expendable if they don't contribute to economic boom.[3]

The double narrative structure of the film (two stories, interlocked) allows us to view the primary love story, that of Count Almásy and Katharine Clifton, by the perspective of the secondary story, which is a story about profound healing—*healing* in the biblical sense, as "signs of the incoming Kingdom of God."[4]

GOING TO THE MOVIES

The English Patient
Anthony Minghella, 1996, 162 min.; R

When the film begins, the firepower of war and economics appears to have won the day. The little group that gathers in and around the Tuscan villa where nurse Hana shelters her burn patient are the castoffs of a civilization that had once professed to love God, Schubert, and good deeds. What are their chances against a power-mad world? Not much, it seems. How this little group changes the terms by which "victory" would be defined, how it renews, refreshes, and rebuilds, is the drama we enter when in the opening sequence of the movie we first see blood-red figures of swimmers being painted across our screen.

PLOT *The English Patient* tells among its interlocked stories the tales of two romances. One is that of Almásy (Hungarian archaeologist and mapmaker engaged in an international exploration of the North African desert) and Katharine (wife of his colleague, Geoffrey Clifton). Their affair takes place about six years before the romance that develops between Hana, a Canadian nurse, and Kip, a soldier in the British Army. Linking these two love stories is the love Hana bears for her last patient of World War II, a severely burned man with whom she has hidden herself away in a bombed-out villa in Tuscany.

Katharine dies. Hana survives, and through healing others and being loved, she herself is healed.

REFLECTIONS The metaphor of healing permeates the film. The physical healing of war wounds is obvious. But equally as painful as the severed limbs and scorched flesh are the interior wounds: alienation from the self, from God, and from other people and other cultures. Alienation calls out for healing action.

Kip, whose mission with the army is to dismantle hidden explosives, suffers from conflicting national identities: He is Indian, a Sikh, but also more British than the British with whom he works, and more British than his just and fervently religious self dares to admit. Count Almásy (as he appears to us in flashbacks) prides himself in owing allegiance to no country and no god. Hana severs her identity as an army nurse to escape the horror of war's deaths. The thief

Caravaggio (another character in this complex drama, played by Willem Dafoe) is a roving spy and pickpocket. All are wounded.

But the most obvious healing mission is wrapped up in the scorched body of Hana's burn patient. He is a man of indeterminate age and nationality whom his rescuers called "the English patient." He exists profoundly in "story." His history not known, others make up tales about him; they create for him an identity to replace the one that has been burned away. He is himself a "circuitous" storyteller, endlessly garrulous and multilingual, interlacing quotes from Herodotus with his own theories about "Virgilian man."[5]

But whoever he *was* in a past life, he *is* a man whose body has lost all power to protect itself. A small household gathers around him, dedicated to his care despite the medical futility of his situation. He should have died long before, probably within an hour after his small plane crashed. He did not. He fell into the hands of broken healers who are soothed by his tales of his past life, by his virtual interactions with the histories contained in the massive volume of Herodotus he keeps by his bedside, and by his funny commentaries on all their loves and fears and fetishes. Despite his sardonic comment to Hana when she mentions that a new person has materialized (and that the soldiers have arrived in the area)—"We should charge admission"—the healing narrative in the film demands the presence of these particular, representative "others."

"Healing" alone does not create an inherently ethical and theological film, however. What makes this film meaningful are the ways that its healing dimension interweaves with the moral issues the film raises. It does not quite resolve these problems—intentionally so, I believe. These are the same problems that easily could be termed "morally reprehensible."

What is "morally reprehensible" in the film is not its greeting-card sentiments ("cut apart and reassembled into a Cubist construction,"[6] as one commentator put it), sentiments such as these:

> "There is a plant that, if you scoop out its heart, fills up with water by the next morning. . . . Every night I cut out my heart, but in the morning it was full again."
> "We didn't care about boundaries, did we?"
> "Betrayals in love are worse than those in war."
> "What do you hate?" "Ownership. Being owned."
> "Here I'm a different wife."
> "There is no God, but I hope someone looks after you."

There are plenty of these tidy sayings, mostly in the Almásy-Katharine romance plot. But what might be seen as "morally reprehensible" in this film are events and relationships that have consequences—consequences of actions that may have been innocent of evil intent, but that nonetheless have brought harm to other people.

First among the problems is that adultery is seemingly justified where the two parties are passionately in love. Second (for the first point is thoroughly undercut by both images and words) is that good and evil result from random happenings in which human choice plays little role. Third is that revenge and murder may be endorsed if the initial crime is adequately offensive.[7]

The fourth problem involves the backdrop of the movie drama itself—the events leading up to and encompassing World War II. This is a far more complex matter than the first (adultery), but it is intricately enmeshed with the second (a random universe) and third (free-floating revenge). The charge is that "heroic" morality appears to supersede all other types of morality. That is, within the romance/epic narrative, the hero Almásy's surrender of crucial maps of North Africa to the Nazi army is glorified, even justified, because it allows him to "keep a promise" (to his sweetheart, to return to rescue her from the swimmer's cave). In his view, everyone is equal in war, and it doesn't matter in the final analysis who gets killed as long as "the [heroic] code" is preserved.

A fifth matter could trouble some viewers: Hana, the nurse, administers a supposedly lethal dose of morphine to her patient on his request, thus allowing him to die by double effect.[8]

In the background lies a challenge to "law" itself: the perception that in wartime or away from your own country or out of the confines of your own social structure, you are free to do as you want.[9] You are a "different kind of wife"—Katharine's words about herself—or you can have a "different kind of love"—a phrase used by a married explorer to justify his affair with one of the young male workers in the expedition.

These are two examples of breaches of private morality. But public morality is also under examination. The film is infused with images of and references to colonialism. World War II marked the end of the golden age of colonialism, and part of the drama of the contemporary narrative is created by the picture of a shell of a man, the burn patient, sharing food and stories (from the colonial past, represented in the film by Rudyard Kipling's novel *Kim*) with one of Britain's colonials, the competent soldier Kip. In the years before the war, however, colonialism was still in place. With colonialism came the assumption that in the colonies, the "superior" people could do as they wished with their subjects, whom they regarded as inferior in status and personhood.[10] When you were out of your own country, a "different" morality was in operation.[11]

War itself is known to bring about similar dislocations of moral behavior. In wartime, men and women often behave in ways that they could never live with if they were back home. (Killing, rape, and theft, in fact, would be severely punished back home in peacetime.)

These are some of the problems that arise in the film and that continue to trouble viewers long after they have left the theater. But this is part of what makes the movie a timely religious text: its ambiguities, its suggestiveness, and the seriousness of the issues it raises.

INFRACTIONS *The English Patient* exists in a climate of infractions. The volume of Herodotus's *The Histories* that Count Almásy carries with him at all times is a complicated sign of those transgressions. It tells the stories of endless wars and exploitations of the earth, including that of the desert where Almásy and his colleagues now carry on their (supposedly) benign explorations.

The book also has become the journal of its owner: Almásy uses it to record observations on stories past and present, including his own. A photo of him as a child is included. So is a short poem on love that he wrote on the back of a candy wrapper at a Christmas party.[12] So are drawings of tiny red swimmers—copied by his lover, Katharine, from the wall of the cave that Almásy discovered. Each new entry embellishes the older stories, of which it now becomes a part.

In the film's complicated time structure, both the histories and the embellishments link the present time, when the burn patient is dying, with a past time. A set of correspondences across centuries is set up early in the film.[13] The rumpled sheets of the patient's bed sometimes transmute into the undulating terrain upon which he in his memory now roves. The thud of Hana's shoes against the earth outside the patient's window (she is playing hopscotch, a reversion to her childhood) sends the suffering man back into his past. The sounds become the drums at night in the desert, as the exploration team gather around a campfire to sing and tell tales.

The camera cuts once more to the present, where Hana is reading aloud from *The Histories* the story of Candaules, his queen, and her lover, Gyges. Suddenly, without prelude, Hana's voice becomes Katharine's, and an instant later we see Katharine in all her golden, seductive beauty as she tells Candaules's story to the rapt group around the campfire. We do not hear in the film that Almásy is falling in love with her, as we do in the book. ("With the help of an anecdote . . . I fell in love. Words . . . they have power.") Instead, we actually *see* the Count falling in love, as the camera zooms in on his spellbound face. We see Katharine's husband's nervous reaction to the tension in the air. When the camera tracks back out to a medium-distance shot, we can see in one frame all the participants in the new drama and witness Herodotus's story of betrayal taking place once again.

Such an intimate linking of past and present, romantic and realistic narrative, is critical. In a list of infractions that range from adultery to betrayal to killing, the first may seem the smallest. Yet the love affair of Almásy and Katharine, however beautifully their encounters are filmed, forges the first link in a chain of events that will lead to multiple deaths: Katharine's, her husband's, and the thousands killed when the Nazis enter Tobruk. The love story of Candaules's queen and Gyges is told in Herodotus without moral judgment: Candaules is killed, and Gyges, who takes his place, rules without incident for twenty-eight years. Almásy's and Katharine's story is not "heroic," however. What they do has consequences for others.

Almásy is portrayed in the movie as a man of integrity— strong, silent, and upright, like the heroes of Greek drama, knights of medieval romance, or avengers of American Westerns. Although he takes pains to surround himself with international colleagues, his own national origin cannot be denied. He is from Hungary, proud land with a language related to no other, a fiercely independent nation that, like the desert in which Almásy now works, repeatedly has suffered invasion and appropriation by powerful armies and kings.

It is partly Almásy's heroic stature that allows the film to be completely dominated by his personality and his quests.[14] He is strongly identified with the graceful swimming figures that we see in the opening sequence of the film; not only does he discover the cave in which these figures are painted, but his life resembles that of an elegant athlete. He moves easily over terrain that is death to most others; he has learned the languages and the coping skills that allow him to penetrate the desert's secrets. He has also absorbed the lessons of long-vanished cultures, and he respects the knowledge of contemporary cultures generally ignored by the West (such as that of the Bedouins, with whom he is able to converse in their native tongue).

Almásy, that is to say, is a man of integrity who also has a firm vocation. One note about that vocation: It is unfair to criticize the Count's mapping team as "polyglot," as one critic has done, since a knowledge of many languages (including the arcane) is essential to unlocking the secrets of the past. This point is made comfortably in *Raiders of the Lost Ark* and *Stargate*, adventure films that feature heroes who include in their mastery of multiple languages dead ones such as Latin, Attic Greek, Sanskrit, and hieroglyphics—just to name a few. These are tools of the trade, like the six-gun or the sword and shield. That Indiana Jones in *Raiders* also wields a mean bullwhip adds to box-office receipts, no doubt, but nonetheless, the movie heavily emphasizes that he is a professor at one of the greatest research universities in the world—the University of Chicago! *Doctor* Jones is shown teaching a large class of delighted undergraduates before he is recruited for his next James Bond-style adventure. Being smart isn't a liability, nor is knowing a lot of languages, if your vocation (and your survival) depend upon access to parts of the world where English is not spoken.[15]

Most suggestively, there is emotional appeal to witnessing the flowering of love in the desert in two arid hearts: Almásy's and Katharine's. Nonetheless, although its narrative is so strongly oriented toward acknowledging and applauding that love, it is hard to realize that *the film does not in fact endorse that love without qualification;* neither does it excuse Almásy's subsequent actions as "justified" by his great passion.

Furthermore, the love is undercut in part by Almásy's own code of honor, which leads him at first to distance himself from Katharine by calling her "Mrs. Clifton" and by refusing to accept her gift of the cave-drawings. When Katharine takes the initiative and comes to his room in the hotel over the *souk* (market), he rips her dress—the stuff of melodrama, perhaps, but not a mark of tenderness, and a clear violation of respect for a woman's body.

The relationship, increasingly marked by pain, is pointedly compared with the affair of Almásy's colleague with a young man in their caravan. Just as that young man knocks his head on an opening within the cave, so also Katharine knocks her head against a support beam (in the scene where she breaks up with Almásy). Gone are the novel's references to the actual bites and other wounds inflicted by Katharine on Almásy, but still present are the life-destroying marks of obsession. Almásy cannot do without her presence; she, in turn, is being consumed by the battle between her passion and her conscience.

We can't escape the questions posed in this particular part of the movie. Does the story of Almásy and Katharine help us work out how we should live?[16] Are we meant to deplore their actions or applaud them as substitutes for our own quite ordinary romances and dreams? The questions raised by this romance have to do with human desires, the search for self-fulfillment. These desires are variously shown as the need to be alone and self-sufficient, to be free (to move, to think, to not be "possessed"), conflicting with equally strong needs for physical release: the need to be loved, to be in companionship, to be understood, to be *cherished*.

However, the conflict between personal need and the needs of the larger society (the law; public opinion; the sanctity of the marriage bond) is not ignored. Katharine's words "I can't do this anymore" refer quite unmistakably to her adulterous relationship with Almásy. She is visibly ill from the effort of maintaining a relationship that must remain secret. What is unspoken is her affection for her husband. They are lifelong friends. Their history, revealed in brief snatches throughout the movie, lies behind her words: "I can't do this." To her, her affair is a "betrayal in love" so painful that she must choose *another* betrayal — of the one whom she loves outside the law.

In *The English Patient*, adultery is far from being glamorized. Those keen to find literary references inside films may pick up the references to Tolstoy's *Anna Karenina*, a novel that hardly romanticizes adulterous liaisons. Rather, it relates the story of a woman who in guilt, loneliness, and despair throws herself under a train.

The Count defines the law according to his own code, however. The only "betrayal in love" is Katharine's, by no longer cleaving to him as his wife. The Count's quest for knowledge has been displaced by his quest for perfect ownership. He is like the person of whom Kierkegaard writes:

> It is blessed to love, to be reduced to a single desire. What does it matter if all other desires are fulfilled or denied? There is but one desire, the loved one; one longing, the loved one; one possession, the loved one! We laud the happiness of love.

But, Kierkegaard continues,

> It is not so ordered that this should be the highest thing of all.[17]

That one thing, the "highest thing of all," as Kierkegaard relates, is to will the good, which is "purity of heart" — single-minded devotion to God.

Kierkegaard's thoughts are very much to the point with *The English Patient*. Almásy, the hero of the romance-epic part of the movie, resembles the alienated hero of Dostoyevsky's *Crime and Punishment*. Almásy's inner conflicts are captured in his exchange with Madox, his colleague and best friend, before Madox leaves Egypt to return to England. Almásy says to his dear friend, "I don't believe in God, but I hope someone looks after you."

Up to this time, Madox and Almásy have been united in friendship and common quest. Madox, sensing that his friend is in danger, has warned him against becoming involved with Katharine. When Madox hears that Almásy has turned over their expedition maps to the Nazis, he kills himself. It is Almásy, the lover of humanity, who brings about the death of his closest friend. This is no fault of a punishing or inattentive Providence; this is the result of human decision.

REDEMPTION As heroic and romantic drama, the events in the distant narrative of *The English Patient* are deeply moving. This part of the film's story drives toward the moment when we see Almásy from a distance, carrying Katharine's body out of the cave and raising his voice in a howl toward the empty heavens. This is material for Sophocles or Shakespeare. The director suppresses the sound of that howl, leaving our imaginations to resonate with this man's indescribable grief—a howl at unbearable loss that I once heard from a dear friend at his little son's graveside; a howl against a universe that seems hostile to human desires.

But that howl is also the cry of Job or of Jesus on the cross. Despite the movie's apparently secular setting, it exists within a larger framework of divine command and covenant: that we shall love the Lord our God with all our heart and soul and mind, and love our neighbor as ourselves (see Matthew 22:37-39). A spectator might bring that perspective to a viewing of the film and see Almásy's grief unsympathetically. However, the film itself provides moral reflection through the healing narrative, in which troublesome issues left unresolved in the romantic part of the film are worked through in present "real" time.

It is in the present time that we see the consequences of Almásy's actions. We learn not only that Caravaggio's mutilation resulted from the Nazi penetration of the desert (with the help of Almásy's maps), but also that thousands of people died as a result. Katharine and her husband died because of Almásy's love affair. Almásy's best friend kills himself from shame. Almásy himself suffers injuries worse than death. Like the bombs and mines hidden by the retreating German army, which continue to inflict a legacy of death upon the innocent, the infractions in the past retain the power to maim and kill.

There is an eerie visual correspondence between the blood-red stick figures of the swimmers painted on the walls of the cave, which suggest the prehistory of a moist earth turned parched and barren, and the body of the once-vibrant Katharine, now turned to bones and dust. The romance has brought death, not life.

Out of death comes life, as the overarching story of present healing reinterprets Almásy's past story. The Bedouin medicine man who first treated the burn patient, and nurse Hana, who took over the patient's care, are both resourceful healers. Water, a luxury craved—and obtained—by the wealthy Katharine (as in the scene where she bathes with her lover), is precious to Hana, her patient, and their gathered household. To Hana, water means purity, as she seeks to cleanse from her suffering heart the memory of young men and women blown to pieces in this inhuman war. It also means life for her patient, whose scorched body requires constant vigilance to prevent life-threatening evaporation of vital fluids. The patient craves water to replenish what he loses; he also is in great need of forgiveness of sins and baptism into new life.

The oddest purification rites occur within this remote villa, shoved "outside the camp" by the necessities of wartime. The patient voices a need: "I miss the rain on my face." His motley crew of caregivers, all outcasts—a nurse/deserter, a thief, a cockney, and a displaced Sikh soldier—race their patient, their adopted child, outside into the pouring rain on a dark and stormy night. They are as thirsty for cooling rain as he is.

Ironically, the patient is "confessed" by a thief, Caravaggio, who has dared to pose to the patient the questions of identity and moral responsibility: "Who are you?" and "Did you kill the Cliftons?" It is Caravaggio who hears the rambling stories of which we are the visual witnesses, and Caravaggio who finally stands at the patient's window, looking out into the night, and pronounces the dying man forgiven. It is he, too, who hears the confession for which the patient has kept himself alive: that yes, he does bear responsibility for the deaths of the people he loved.

This scene of absolution ("I can't kill you now") could be criticized as letting the patient off the hook for his crimes. But by this time in the film, healing as a *need* and healing as an *action* have been set firmly in place to counter its ethical opposite: endless and endlessly refined revenge. What is the appropriate response to tragedy—to hunt down and kill the enemy, as Caravaggio did with the people who cut off his thumbs, and as John Wayne in *The Searchers* did with the Comanches? To resign oneself to the passive suffering of wrong as inevitable? Both of these responses give evil a front seat in the universe.

The responses suggested in the present-day narrative of the film are creative, not despairing. Hana, broken by endless loss, retreats from the war but immediately begins planting vegetables, restoring humanity to her patient, and giving love to Kip. Kip, even though he has been marginalized by the British society he fights to preserve, continues to dismantle bombs—another activity of healing and redemption. He is a purifier of the earth but also an agent in Hana's inner healing. He is fearless and gentle; his purity of heart (both as single-mindedness and as innocence) is unquestioned; he gains nothing for himself in coming so far from home to save the lives of men whose country has bound his own. He asks for nothing from Hana in return for her love.[18]

Kip's generosity in love contrasts strikingly with Almásy's. Where Almásy's love for Katharine is marked by fierce obsession and possession, Kip's response to Hana's love is to light her way through the garden in the night, and then to use his skills with block and tackle to hoist her to the top of an ancient church to rejoice in its exquisite frescoes.

How to heal the wounds of war—the ravaged terrain, the shattered bodies, the crushed spirits? *Touch* heals; *love*, generously shared, heals; *community of care* heals; *art* heals. But what about the wounds of domination? The film provides images for this kind of healing. Hana is fully immersed in work— physical, dirty, bloody work. The dislocations of war demand a gender-free consignment of tasks, and in retreat, she is shown working the earth, bringing life out of death. Katharine Clifton and the other expatriate men and women can be cool and idle and well-fed because their (doomed) lifestyle rests on the labor of others—the silent servants standing at attention behind the diners; those who cook for the Christmas feast, whose labors take place in hot, confined interiors; servants who ride on the tops of the explorers' jeeps, fully exposed to the brutal sun.

But through Hana, work is not devalued; it is elevated. The intelligence of the Count, the focused revenge of the thief, the concentrated evil of the soldiers who planted the hidden bombs are no match for Hana's miracles as she transforms the shell of a villa into a home for the homeless: a home with a garden, scarecrow, orchard, kitchen, canopied bed, and community room—and a sickroom that even becomes a ballroom.

The author of one article scorns the movie's talk about internationalism: "What's really celebrated in this film is not . . . internationalism but a moral and spiritual isolationism."[19] In Hana's—and Kip's—narrative, however, internationalism is presented carefully as our mutual life within the body of God—a suffering, displaced, burned, or despised body, perhaps, but a beautiful one nevertheless because it is *human*. The faces of saints, queens, and prophets that Hana sees on the wall of the chapel resemble the faces of Hana, Kip, and all the other persons we see in the film. The members of this household in the outcast villa live together in "covenant fidelity" (Karl Barth), protecting and caring for one another in an extended family. The common (communion) room where we see Kip and the patient share condensed milk and where all share wine is both *enclosed* and *open*; its walls are still intact, but its bombed-out windows let in the light and air.

Healing comes to all within this little household. For the English patient, it is as though he stayed alive for the moment of confession when he accepts his responsibility for the deaths he caused. As Kierkegaard once wrote, "There is a silent, sleeping sorrow at the picturing at what has been wasted. . . . There is a laborious moving forward in the Good that is like the gait of one whose feet are without skin." The English patient is Kierkegaard's sufferer:

> [W]hen punishment itself becomes a blessing, when consequences even become redemptive, when progress in the Good is apparent; then is there a milder but deep sorrow that remembers the guilt. It has wearied out and overcome what could deceive and confuse the sight.[20]

The "progress in the Good" has been the patient's long months of excruciating pain, where he cannot bear to look at the light; cannot bear the slightest weight on his body; swallows, breathes, and digests with difficulty.

In health, Almásy was intense, silent, risk-taking, self-assigned to probe one of the earth's most mysterious expanses of terrain. In this modern version of Dante's hell, he has been suitably imprisoned for adultery, murder without intent, and betrayal. He is no longer free to chart his own course, never alone, always surrounded by strangers, burning up, and starving to death. This master of words and languages who rarely spoke, as Katharine once observed, now speaks endlessly, with the erudition and edgy sarcasm of the British university man he is thought to be, puncturing the horror of his and the war-torn world's condition with humorous understatement.

Almásy is known, loved, and forgiven, an extreme case, like the thief on the cross. He dies in God's body, not his own, in a time that has been transformed into God's redeeming time.

QUESTIONS 1. What are the implications of the film's using a burn patient rather than some other kind of patient? Treatment of the burn patient has been an issue at the heart of discussions of medical ethics for several decades, in part because of Dax, a severely burned man who pleaded from the first moments of his catastrophe to be allowed to die. It is a continuing question, for instance with the survivors of the Korean airline crash in August of 1997, all of whom were terribly burned. Does a patient have the right to exercise "autonomy" and declare whether he wishes to live or die? Or is life to be prolonged at any cost? Are these even the right questions to ask? Dax said, "I am a dead man," in the sense that he had already experienced the death of the self. As William F. May has written, the wounds caused by severe burning "destroy the soul's clothing and leave the frail self in naked agony."[21]

2. In the novel, Kip's struggle with his allegiance to a country (England) that historically colonized and frequently killed his own people comes into focus when the Allies drop the atomic bomb on Hiroshima and Nagasaki.[22] The injuries sustained by the English patient are like those of the civilian survivors in Japan, or like those suffered in Dresden, Germany, during the firebombing assault on civilian areas at the end of World War II.[23] Do you think the film makes this connection? How?

3. Different styles of healing can be explored as these arise from different concepts of the human self. What becomes of the inner identity when the outer markets of the self—face and functions—are completely gone?

4. Does the film recognize that the English patient in some sense "dies" when his flesh is seared away? The natural response even among health-care givers is to be revolted by the sight of a burn patient, so hideous and threatening are the wounds. Does the film (which is operating, after all, in a general movie climate in which strange-looking aliens are commonplace) "normalize" the sight of the patient's face, when in fact such patients are shocking to look at? Has the director sensationalized this very private agony?

5. What do you make of the ways movies shape audience reaction to sensitive issues? For instance, Caravaggio accuses the English patient of causing the deaths of thousands of people when he turned over valuable exploration maps to the Nazis. The patient responds: "Thousands did die. Just different ones." By this point in the movie, the patient has been made a highly sympathetic character. What are we to make of his words that his betrayal (giving the maps of the desert to the Nazis) did not matter because all people are equally expendable? Are we supposed to adopt his position on the war, that it was wrong *only* because "boundaries" are artificially created and limit the work of "pure" science?

6. Do you find the film's healing elements as strong as its tragic ones? Discuss.

LEADING A FILM STUDY GROUP

The chapters in this book provide different models for ways to explore movies with a group. The suggestions that follow fall into three general areas: how to organize your group; how to select films that fit your group's particular needs; and how to show films and lead group discussions using this book.

One of the most important tasks in starting a film study group is deciding what you consider to be "religious" films—and where you want to draw the boundaries for the discussions you will undertake. My personal movie choices begin with an assumption that the material of life—our thresholds, our passages—is by its nature religious. I feel that any movie that takes human concerns seriously is appropriate for discussion in a religious setting.

Turn this idea around. Films may be classified as religious not so much by their obvious subject matter (the Ten Commandments or the life of Jesus, for instance) as by viewers' careful attention to the characters' struggles to live well and understand themselves, and to how the movie reflects and/or addresses human values and life concerns. A religious movie challenges and stretches its viewers. Thoughtful reading of a film blossoms when you help to establish a spirit of group covenant and respect. Eat together, pray together, watch together, reflect together, argue and support your assertions! You will create a dynamic spirit that will carry over from group meetings into independent viewings.

Planning the Film Study Group

Time and Place

1. How often does your group want to meet—weekly, monthly, or "occasionally" (i.e., will this become a regular series, or will you meet as occasion demands)? How long do you need for each meeting or session—one hour, two hours, three hours or more? Do you want to include mealtime as part of your meetings? How many weeks or months do you want to continue meeting; do you want to meet for a year or more?

2. Sunday morning sessions may be brief, but they can also be fruitful. The group leader might assign a film for class members to view before the next Sunday, then rely on class members' memories (aided by film clips) to guide the discussion. This plan has proved workable when the leader provides questions in advance of the group meeting to guide private reflection. Class discussion can be designed to focus on issues that would interest everyone in the class, even those who have not yet seen the film.

3. Ideally, your group will be able to view films *together*. The communal experience is important, and memories will be fresh. Evening meetings can be successful and even addictive! There are several models—including a shorter session (approximately two hours—includes viewing the film and having a short discussion) and a longer session (film, brief meal, discussion). If possible, make time for the leader to introduce the film and to suggest a few questions to consider when viewing. Take a short break after watching the film

to allow for reflection. Allow plenty of time after the movie for discussion.

4. If you are not able to schedule time to view the film as a group, be sure to review the plot together before you begin discussion. This will allow everyone to start the discussion with the basic facts in mind.

5. If possible, plan a group trip to a movie theater. The full impact of a film is best felt when it is seen in a theater, with its wide-screen format, state-of-the-art sound system, and communal atmosphere.

Group Composition

1. What is the composition of your group by age, gender, occupation, hobbies, prior movie-viewing experience, and religious orientation? What differences may exist if you come from diverse backgrounds or cultural experiences?

2. Do your members prefer to meet with others of their own age? (Age may help determine movie choices, particularly for teens or young adults. Older adults may not enjoy films with much violence, but they may relish other mainstream fare. Recently, a group of octogenarians attended a screening of *Home Alone 3* and enjoyed it immensely!)

3. Do you want to encourage religious and cultural diversity within your group? Persons with varied travel or life experiences may pick up visual or verbal cues in a movie that others miss. Another purpose of your film group might be to share different perspectives on life's passages.

Group Leadership

1. What will the group leader's role be? Do group members want to share the responsibility of preparing for sessions?

2. What learning style would work best for the group—focused study, casual conversation, or a combination of these? If this is to be a study group, how much advance preparation are members willing to commit to?

3. Who will be in charge of or assist with the film-viewing equipment?

Selecting Films

Group Purpose

What is your purpose in meeting as a group; what do you envision for the entire experience? Give some thought to the ways in which fellowship and keen analysis can flourish side by side. Choose films that will highlight the concerns you identify. Discuss the following questions, as needed, with your group:

1. Do you wish to explore theological themes (*theology* is the study of the nature of God and religious truth), paired with Bible study?

2. Are you eager to examine theological implications of movies as a medium, looking at the ways movies may shape our ideas and reactions and influence the ways we interpret history?

3. Do you want to focus on pastoral concerns such as tradition and family?

4. Do you want to think about the spirituality of film as a contemporary art form? (This was the subject of a recent Lenten series, "Art and Soul.")

5. Are you concerned about the ways sex, violence, and language are represented in contemporary movies? This would be a good topic to kick off a movie series. Face these concerns upfront, *before* you make movie selections. Some

of the best contemporary movies that deal with life, vocational choice, religious struggles, and death also may have strong language *(Good Will Hunting)* or violence *(Mean Streets; Fargo; L.A. Confidential)* or explicit sexual content or situations *(Chasing Amy; In the Company of Men)*. You will have to decide whether the honesty, beauty, and religious sensitivity of these films outweigh what some group members may consider to be offensive.

Group Benefit

1. Our thoughts about other cultures are formed in part by what we see on the screen. It is important that we learn to read visual messages carefully. One instructive idea for a film group might be to view a movie that is set in a country that some of your congregation members plan to visit, perhaps on a mission trip. Offer ideas about what to look for on your trip. For instance, if you plan to visit an African country, view and discuss *Daughters of the Dust; Romero* and *The Mission* should be essential viewing for those who will travel to Central or South America; *Wedding in Galilee* is one of the few movies that look at Middle East tensions both fairly and from the inside.

2. Is your group concerned about ethics in politics, business, or personal life? Consider meeting the concerns and needs of special focus groups within your congregation: professionals, life stages, common interests, or assignments. For instance, members who work together on the church newsletter might profit from seeing and discussing the ethical issues in *Broadcast News*. Young female professionals might find *Working Girl* both stimulating and disturbing. *In the Company of Men* may open up a discussion of business ethics, including corporate and personal motivations.

Film Choices

Do you want to view only current, American-made movies or extend your study to include classic and foreign films?

1. The possibilities for expanded study experiences have multiplied wonderfully since the advent of video. As I have suggested earlier in this book, it is a healthy and enlightening experience to study American mainstream films together with films from other industries (independents, foreign, etc.).

2. The images of women's lives, dreams, and hopes are portrayed quite differently in American and foreign films, even today. Mainstream American films today are not so easily pegged as "chick flicks" (films whose primary appeal is to women) or "action hero" movies (think Stallone, Schwarzenegger, Bruce Willis). I encourage any group interested in women's issues to consider varying their movie selections with offerings from France, Germany, Australia, or China.

3. American filmmakers rarely make movies that treat religious faith or community with depth and seriousness (*The Apostle, Kundun,* and *Places in the Heart* being welcome exceptions). However, other film cultures are less hesitant to broach religious questions openly. It is refreshing to look at films where the director has acknowledged religion as a power in daily life, such as *Life on a String* (China); *A Time to Live and a Time to Die* (Taiwan); or *Taste of Cherry* (Iran).

4. Silent films can inspire rich discussions of religious issues in a social context. Consider such silent-film treasures as *Metropolis; The Passion of Joan of Arc; Greed; Sunrise;* or *Intolerance.*

5. Expand upon the types of films you use. Try comedy. Try documentaries such as *Hoop Dreams* or *Four Little Girls*

(Spike Lee, 1997). Consider films with more relaxed story-telling styles. Try independent films (such as *Ulee's Gold* or *The Apostle*), which often raise important life issues in fresh ways because the story has not been washed out by marketing or financial concerns.

Outside Opinions

1. Search the library, the Internet, books, newspapers, and trade magazines for reviews and discussions of the film you are going to view. Does the film elicit positive, useful, or searching reflections?

2. Does the film trigger anger or dismay? Don't be turned off by negative reviews! *The Last Temptation of Christ* and *Jesus of Montreal,* for instance, puzzled and infuriated some people when they were originally released. Both *Kundun* and *The Apostle* have been criticized as well. Nonetheless, all four films are serious attempts by talented filmmakers to explore religious faith and may work well with your group.

Showing and Discussing Films

Preparing for Viewing and Discussion

1. Choose a chapter or part of a chapter in this book that speaks to you. Suggest ways for the class to think about the material in the chapter.
2. In what ways is the discussion in this chapter captivating or useful? What questions does the discussion raise? What questions need to be answered?
3. How might the discussion be expanded to more fully explore the film the class will view together? What curiosities do you have about the film?

4. How does the approach in this chapter apply to other films you have seen?

5. Prepare a few questions for the group to hang their thoughts on as you watch the film together.

Showing Films

NOTE: Be aware that all motion pictures are protected by copyright law. There are certain legal requirements that you must adhere to in the public showing and viewing of films, and *these requirements apply to both for-profit and nonprofit organizations, including churches and church-affiliated groups.* Before showing or viewing any movie, review carefully "The Fine Print" (in appendix 2) for a briefing of the applicable copyright law and a related list of frequently asked questions and answers. It is the sole responsibility of each individual or group to be aware of and comply with any and all applicable copyright laws.

1. First, decide upon a viewing format. Videocassettes are still the most widely used and easiest-to-rent format. The laserdisc and digital video disc (DVD) formats offer superior film and sound quality, but they are also more expensive—both the necessary viewing equipment and the discs themselves. And there are currently very few film titles available for rent in these formats. Perhaps some of your group members own a laserdisc or DVD player and one or more of the films you choose to view; this would provide a different viewing experience and possibly a pleasant change of pace and environment for your group.

2. Be sure to test your viewing equipment before you make a presentation. If you are using a videocassette player (VCR), be sure to have a special tape called a "head cleaner" in case the VCR has been heavily used and needs clean-

ing. (A dirty machine will give you a fuzzy, snowy picture.)
Follow the instructions included with your head cleaner for
its use.

3. Use a hand-held remote control with your viewing equipment, if available; this allows you to move freely about the
meeting area as you show the film.

4. If you are showing a selected "clip"—a short segment of the
film—have it pre-cued and ready to play. If you are showing more than one clip, be sure you know exactly where to
find each clip on the tape. (Using a VCR with a counter is
helpful; discs are usually indexed by segments and are rel-
atively easy to access.)

5. If you are showing a film with subtitles, it would be helpful
to provide the group with a plot synopsis and a few guides
to understanding the film. Be sure that the subtitles can be
easily read.

6. Use a TV monitor or viewscreen that is large enough for
everyone to see a clear image; consider using a video pro-
jector if you don't have an adequate screen but have a large,
flat, light-colored surface such as a wall.

7. Check the audio source on your equipment prior to the
group meeting. Make sure that the sound is clear, easy-to-
hear and understand, and that the volume can be turned to
an adequate level. Keep in mind that group members may
have different hearing capabilities and needs. Find a volume level that everyone is comfortable with—not too loud,
and not too soft. Group members may want to seat themselves closer to the speaker or farther away, depending
upon their hearing capabilities, needs, or preferences.

8. ALWAYS pre-screen the film you will show—watch it well
in advance of the group viewing, so you will be prepared to
plan the session, answer questions, or choose another film
if necessary.

Movie-Rental Sources

1. Check your local video-rental store(s). The major video-rental chain stores will have many or all of the films examined in this book, or will be able to order them for you to purchase.

2. Try your local library; even small libraries may have good video collections or can obtain a number of films through interlibrary loan. Some offer video rentals at no charge.

3. Check the Internet; you should be able to find information about movie-rental companies, including specialty stores, as well as movies for sale. Try the Home Film Festival website (*www.homefilmfestival.com*); also, the Internet Movie Database (*us.imdb.com*) has information about movies for sale and is a great research tool.

4. Facets Multimedia, 1517 W. Fullerton, Chicago, IL, 60614-2087, rents a wide array of videos for a reasonable fee. They will send the videos directly to you.

5. Last, if you are having trouble finding movies for rental, consider purchasing them for your group; this would depend on the cost of the particular films, whether your group will be ongoing or only temporary, your group's expense budget, and whether you want to start and/or maintain a film library.

Guiding and Building Group Discussion

The following questions are designed to open up avenues for fuller exploration of the movies you watch together. As group leader, reflect on these questions and discuss, as needed, with your group:

1. In what ways is this a great film? What are the important religious or ethical questions or issues that it raises? How is this film like or unlike my own experiences? How does it

represent events and people that are unfamiliar? Is this done with curiosity and respect for another ethnic group, religion, or culture?

2. What response does the film elicit toward the persons shown in this film—condescending, judgmental, puzzled, curious, or compassionate? How might the events in the film help me to understand myself or other persons more fully? Is this a film that stimulates compassion and encourages a listening heart?

3. What issues surface in this movie? (Examples: interracial dating; child abuse; parent-child relationship; sexual orientation; delivery of health care; citizen-police interaction; environmental concerns; education.) Are you satisfied with the way the movie's issues are handled? How might the director of the film have explored the central issues more completely?

4. Films differ in the amount of information they supply about the characters' lives and the events that occurred before the movie begins. Do you know enough about the background of the film's characters and events (its *fabula* world) to understand what you see on the screen (the *story*)? What would you like to know, and why might this be helpful? How does the film fill in the gaps in your knowledge about the characters' histories and secrets? Do you want to know more, or does the absence of information serve some purpose in the movie as a whole?

5. Classical drama puts a value on unity of time, place, and action. Some movies follow this formula; most do not, although many present a story with clear time limitations *(Speed, Crimson Tide, Air Force One)*.

How does the way your film uses time or place affect the way you react to the story? For example, *The Apostle* emphasizes the communal nature of religious celebration by using a large percentage of long- or medium-distance shots that allow the entire congregation to be seen at once. At the same time, the film's setting—first Texas, then Louisiana—associates its story with the distinctiveness of the cultures in those two states (compared, for instance, with the Midwest or large cities on the East Coast or West Coast).

6. In many of the best movies, the plot ends are not completely resolved. Why might this be a strength in a movie? What benefits would this have for the viewer? Is the ending of this film open or closed? Is the ending strong? Why or why not? Many movies—*Blade Runner*, for instance—have their endings changed before they are released. Could you imagine your movie redone with a different ending—the priest in *Diary of a Country Priest* saved by a miracle of medical science, for instance, or sisters Karin and Maria permanently reconciled in *Cries and Whispers*? How would this change your view of the movie as a whole?

7. Classical Hollywood editing is designed to be invisible; you are hardly aware you are seeing a movie. Is this a film that seems to distort or change what you see? What do these changes add to the film? How do they hurt the film?

8. Sound can be a powerful stimulant, influencing the interpretation of what you are seeing. A well-made film uses music and sound with care and purpose. How is sound used in this movie? What sounds other than music are you aware of (for example, street sounds, a train, machinery, and so forth)? Many films (if not most) use music in some purposeful way: 1960s rock 'n' roll and soul music in *The Big Chill*; 1950s music for *American Graffiti*; convoluted piano noodlings in *The Piano*; or grating, eerie, repetitive music in *Vertigo*. Does the music enhance or overwhelm the dialogue or the story?

9. A movie's story may be told in many different ways. It may be *linear* (one event follows another in a straight line; all events are connected) or *episodic* (events are not necessarily connected) or *responsive* (the connection between events may be in how other persons respond to what has already been said or done). A story may also be punctuated by flashbacks, dream sequences, or fantasies. And more than one storyline may be unrolling in the same film.

   Ask: How is this movie's story being told? How does the way the story is being told affect the ways you understand the story itself? Is there more than one storyline? Are the stories of equal importance?

10. A director may choose major film stars (such as Tom Cruise or Julia Roberts) or lesser-known actors (such as Guy Pearce and Russell Crowe in *L.A. Confidential*) or may use nonprofessional actors (as in *Taste of Cherry*). Ask: Is this a film with major stars? If so, do you feel the choice of star power (generally or in particular) helps or harms the movie? Does the use of a major star highlight or overshadow the issues you consider important in the movie? How? What are the advantages of using nonprofessionals or unknown actors?

11. Is there a "moment of understanding" or clarification in this film? What is it? In many films, a key speech opens all eyes: Spencer Tracy's in *Inherit the Wind* and again in *Guess Who's Coming to Dinner?* Clarence the angel's final lecture in *It's a Wonderful Life*; or the father's sermon after his son has died in *A River Runs Through It*. Do you feel satisfied or cheated by the film's ending? Why?

   Voice-over is another way a director may seek to control your interpretation of events in the movie. Do you agree with the observations and opinions expressed in the voice-over? Why or why not?

12. Many contemporary movies are remakes of older versions or fall within a known story type such as science fiction, romantic comedy, or the Western. Is this a genre movie? What other films of this type are you familiar with? How does this film differ from the other films of this type that you are familiar with? Why do you think this type of movie has become so popular? What does it have to say about the national culture or religious values?

ADDITIONAL FILMS FOR STUDY

* = listed in the National Film Registry (established by Congress to preserve movies that are "culturally, historically or aesthetically important"); twenty-five films are added each year

** = included on the Vatican's list of the 45 all-time greatest religious, spiritual, or artistic films

Home

Blue (Krzysztof Kieslowski, Poland, 1993)

Days of Heaven (Terrence Malick, 1978)

The Double Life of Veronica (Kieslowski, Poland, 1991)

The Piano (Jane Campion, New Zealand, 1993)

Shadowlands (Richard Attenborough, UK, 1993)

* *Sunrise* (F. W. Murnau, 1927)

Authenticity

The Bridges of Madison County (Clint Eastwood, 1995)

Day of Wrath (Carl-Theodor Dreyer, Denmark, 1943)

Life on a String (Kaige Chen, China, 1991)

Mean Streets (Martin Scorsese, 1973)

Passion Fish (John Sayles, 1992)

Tree of the Wooden Clogs (Ermanno Olmi, Italy, 1978)

Alienation

* *Badlands* (Terrence Malick, 1973)

Un coeur en hiver (A Heart in Winter) (Claude Sautet, France, 1992)

Gattaca (1997)

* *One Flew Over the Cuckoo's Nest* (Milos Forman, 1975)

The Sweet Hereafter, (Atom Egoyan, Canada, 1997)

* *Star Wars* (George Lucas, 1977)

Stalker (Andrei Tarkovsky, USSR, 1979)

Taste of Cherry (Abbas Kiarostami, Iran, 1997)

* *Taxi Driver* (Martin Scorsese, 1976)

* *Vertigo* (Alfred Hitchcock, 1958)

Vocation

Amadeus (Milos Forman, 1984)

An Angel at My Table (Jane Campion, New Zealand, 1990)

Bird (Clint Eastwood, 1988)

* *Citizen Kane* (Orson Welles, 1941)

Dead Man Walking (Tim Robbins, 1995)

Good Will Hunting (Gus Van Sant, 1997)

Hoop Dreams (Steve James II, 1994)

Kundun (Martin Scorsese, 1997)

The Mission (Roland Joffé, UK, 1986)

* *On the Waterfront* (Elia Kazan, 1954)

* *Raging Bull* (Martin Scorsese, 1980)

Winter Light (Ingmar Bergman, Sweden, 1963)

Integrity

Field of Dreams (Phil Alden Robinson, 1989)

* *High Noon* (Fred Zinnemann, 1952)

L.A. Confidential (Curtis Hanson, 1997)

Matewan (John Sayles, 1987)

Mississippi Masala (Mira Nair, 1991)

* *The Outlaw Josey Wales* (Clint Eastwood, 1976)

La Promesse (Dardenne brothers, Belgium, 1996)

A River Runs Through It (Robert Redford, 1992)

Romero (John Duigan, 1989)

Stand By Me (Rob Reiner, 1986)

* *Touch of Evil* (Orson Welles, 1958)

Purity of Heart

Babe (Chris Noonan, 1995)

Being There (Hal Ashby, 1979)

Breaking the Waves (Lars von Trier, Denmark, 1996)

Children of Paradise (Marcel Carné, France, 1945)

** *Flowers of St. Francis* (Roberto Rossellini, Italy, 1950)

** *The Passion of Joan of Arc*
(Carl-Theodor Dreyer,
France, 1928)
* *To Kill a Mockingbird*
(Robert Mulligan, 1962)
Where Is the Friend's Home?
(Abbas Kiarostami, Iran,
1987)

**Celebration
(Conflict and Healing)**

Antonia's Line (Marleen
Gorris, Netherlands, 1995)
As Good as It Gets (James L.
Brooks, 1997)
The Apostle (Robert Duvall,
1997)

Black Orpheus (Marcel
Camus, Brazil, 1959)
Eat Drink Man Woman (Ang
Lee, Taiwan/USA, 1994)
Ikiru (Akira Kurosawa,
Japan, 1952)
It's a Wonderful Life (Frank
Capra, 1946)
Places in the Heart (Robert
Benton, 1984)
Tender Mercies (Bruce
Beresford, 1983)
Smoke (Wayne Wang, 1995)
Wild Strawberries (Ingmar
Bergman, Sweden, 1957)

THE FINE PRINT: COPYRIGHT INFORMATION

Q: I understand that motion pictures are protected by federal copyright laws. Do these copyright laws apply to showing movies with our church's film-study group, or with other church-affiliated groups?

A: Yes. Under the law, for-profit and nonprofit organizations are required to have a public performance license to show movies, which include purchased and rental videocassettes.

Q: How does my church obtain rights to show full-length films and film clips for Christian education purposes?

A: You need to obtain a public performance license (sometimes called a site license or umbrella license) to publicly show movies on home video, even for educational purposes. An umbrella license can be granted by The Motion Picture Licensing Corporation (MPLC). The MPLC's Church Desk handles these requests. Contact Harald Bauer, Executive Vice President, at 800-515-8855 (fax 203-270-8830).

Q: What is an umbrella license, and what does it allow the church to do?

A: An umbrella license is a 12-month license purchased by your church that enables you to use copyrighted films of your choice for preaching and teaching. If your church purchases an umbrella license, you may use entire videos or clips in your film-study group, and your pastor can use clips with sermons.

Q: How much will an umbrella license cost?

A: Generally, the umbrella license costs $95 for a 12-month period.

Q: Are there any less expensive alternatives?

A: Yes. Many denominations—through conferences, jurisdictions, dioceses, and other structures—already have public-performance license agreements for their churches. Under these agreements, the church office negotiates with the MPLC a much lower rate per church. If your church's jurisdiction has an umbrella license for its churches, your church can qualify for the lower rate. If you're not sure, call your church's jurisdictional offices and ask whether an umbrella license agreement exists or is being pursued.

Q: Without an umbrella license, are there ways to incorporate current films with our film-study group?

A: Yes. The information found in this book in the "Leading a Film Study Group" section is applicable to any and all movies. It is up to the group leader and/or group participants to decide which films to view, including from among films currently playing in theaters. Check your local-area newspaper or call the theater for movie listings and showtimes.

Q: Are there other restrictions, even if we purchase an umbrella license?

A: Yes. You may use only prerecorded videos, such as those purchased legally by an individual or those rented from video stores or the public library.

You may not dub selected clips onto another cassette to show to your group—the clip must be cued from the original prerecorded tape. No license exists for showing movies taped from television or cable.

If you have any questions about your legal rights, call The Motion Picture Licensing Corporation at 800-515-8855.

THE COPYRIGHT LAW

- The Copyright Act grants to the copyright owner the exclusive right, among others, "to perform the copyrighted work publicly" (Section 106).

- The rental or purchase of a home videocassette does not carry with it the right "to perform the copyrighted work publicly" (Section 202).

- Home videocassettes may be shown, without a license, in the home to "a normal circle of family and its social acquaintances" (Section 101) because such showings are not "public."

- Home videocassettes may also be shown, without a license, in certain narrowly defined "face-to-face teaching activities" (Section 110.1) because the law makes a specific, limited exception for such showing. *There are no other exceptions.*

- All other showings of home videocassettes are illegal unless they have been authorized by license. Even "performances in 'semipublic' places such as clubs, lodges, factories, summer camps, and schools are 'public performances' subject to copyright control" (Senate Report No. 94-473, page 60; House Report No. 94-1476, page 64).

- Institutions, organizations, companies, or individuals wishing to engage in non-home showings of home videocassettes must secure licenses to do so—regardless of whether an admission or other fee is charged (Section 501). This legal requirement applies equally to profit-making organizations and nonprofit institutions (Senate Report No. 94-473, page 59; House Report No. 94-1476, page 62).

Notes

Preface

1. One of the findings has been how consistently and markedly babies respond to "parentese"—that sing-songy nonsense tone many parents use to talk to their little ones. The insights about children's brains resonates with the words of Martin Buber a half-century ago: "Children, like adults, should be treated as a 'Thou,' someone to be cherished, not an 'It,' something to be used and discarded" (see *I and Thou*).

2. See Robert Coles, *The Moral Intelligence of Children: How to Raise a Moral Child* (New York: Random House, 1997) for an exploration of the power of stories to transmit values and stimulate creative thinking in children.

3. Dorothee Soelle, from a talk at Northwestern University May 15, 1997. The phrase "God has no other hands than our hands" is taken from her book *On Earth as in Heaven* (Westminster John Knox Press, 1993).

How to Use This Book

1. Gunning is professor of film in the Department of Art, University of Chicago. His quote appeared in the University of Chicago alumni magazine in the spring of 1997. I believe Gunning meant, among others, *Sunrise* and *How Green Was My Valley*, both of which appear on his own list of the twelve greatest movies of all time.

Introduction

1. *Adventure, Mystery, and Romance* (Chicago and London: Univ. of Chicago Press, 1976). Paperback, 1977.

2. Margaret Miles makes a similar point when she notes that it is not the subject of a film that makes it "religious," but rather the spectator's "committed and informed imaginative labor." See her insightful book *Seeing*

and Believing: Religion and Values in the Movies (Boston: Beacon Press, 1996).

3. This saying is often overheard at the movies, as if we need to apologize for our entertainment addictions. Thanks to my students in "Women's Issues in Theology," Spring 1997. When they are watched with a critical eye, Hollywood movies can dish up quite complex fare and present spectators with a great deal to worry over. For instance: How can we simultaneously cheer Larry Flynt's crusade for free speech in *The People vs. Larry Flynt* and deplore the disrespect for women that his magazine *Hustler* has promoted? (See M. Miles's article in *Christian Century*, Spring 1997.) How can we root for Luke Skywalker in the *Star Wars* trilogy when (despite Luke's generally admirable persona) "trust the Force" says as much about survival of the fittest and warfare as it says about trust in God?

4. *Breaking the Glass Armor* (Princeton: Princeton Univ. Press, 1988), 12. "Meaning is not the end result of an artwork, but one of its formal components." That is, be careful not to reduce an artwork to a meaning or meanings. I am reminded of a letter my brother-in-law, the artist Richard Vaux, once wrote when I asked what his newest painting "meant": "Don't be concerned with its meanings, enjoy its beauty!" So themes are only part of the interest of the films we will explore in this book.

5. Thanks to Richard Kieckhefer for pointing to this film's simplicity and piety. The director of *Tree* was almost certainly influenced by *Ordet (The Word)*, one of the Danish director Carl Theodor Dreyer's masterworks. *Ordet's* shocking impact (the representation of resurrection onscreen), though it focuses on the power of Christian faith, also probes and affirms the spiritual dimension of all of life.

6. Thanks to Meagan Rawlins, former assistant director of The Fowler Center, Mayville, Michigan.

1. Home

1. *Kieslowski on Kieslowski,* ed. Danusia Stok (London and Boston: Faber & Faber, 1993).

2. A fine study of the cultural and emotional meanings of home is Witold Rybczynski's *Home: A Short History of an Idea* (New York: Penguin, 1986).

3. This scene parallels one that occurs earlier in the film, where Kris falls to the feet of his wife Hari and says, "Forgive me." *Solaris* will be discussed in chapter 3, "Alienation."

4. Ken Vaux reminded me of this hymn we both love, "Once in Royal David's City." From his manuscript in progress: *Eucharistical Theology and the Lord's Prayer,* 1997, 30-1.

5. *Oikos*, the Greek word for "earth," is the basis for ecumenical and economy—"the house."

6. The star Vega in *Contact* is twenty-six light years away from Earth.

7. Amy DeLong first called this movie to my attention.

8. In movies, it is important to separate the *narrative* (what unfolds on the screen) from the *plot* (story summary) and the diegesis or *fabula* (the total world to which the story belongs—the history of the characters, the environment in which they live, the underlying history of this particular time and place). In most movies, it is the contrast between what we see and hear on the screen (narrative) and what we wish we knew *(fabula)* that creates the interest. In a detective movie, much of the excitement hinges on the difference between what we know or *think* we know (based on what we are seeing on the screen) and what is hidden from us (what really happened: crime, love affair, secret history, etc.). David Bordwell defines the *fabula*: "what produces the story, what the story is built upon, and what it refers to" *(Film Art: An Introduction*, 4th ed. [New York: McGraw-Hill, 1993], 90).

9. Movies, like any other type of storytelling, often have a number of purposes. One is simply to "tell the story," which may be similar to or far different from other tellings of the same story. Other reasons might be to explore cultural conflicts *(Mississippi Masala; Lone Star)* or stimulate viewers to think about the nature of violence *(Natural Born Killers, Pulp Fiction)* or to present a nuanced and compassionate exploration of adultery set against the longing for affection *(Bridges of Madison County*, Kieslowski's *Decalogue)*. Cynthia Scott's choice of this particular story reveals a hope that viewers will stretch their ideas about human value and worth.

10. Movie stories don't have to have violent struggles to be compelling. But as Jim Wall and others have pointed out, American films have conditioned us to expect violence and conflict. See James Wall, *Christian Century* (Feb. 26, 1997). This observation is standard in European film criticism: see Jacques Aumont, et al., *Aesthetics of Film* (Austin: Univ. of Texas Press, 1983, trans. Richard Neupert, 1992), 89.

11. Janet Maslin, *New York Times* film critic, used this phrase when she discussed *The Bridges of Madison County* in a 1995 article.

12. *Narrative style* refers to the way in which the movie's story is told: dialogue, monologue, voice-over, flashbacks, and so forth. It also refers to the pace at which the story is told: rapid-fire or edgy, daily, leisurely.

13. Roger Ebert, film critic for the *Chicago Sun-Times*, noted recently that in films where a prisoner awaits death, the governor always waits until the absolute last second to phone in a stay of execution. Otherwise, there would be no suspense. This comment appeared May 18, 1997. See also *Ebert's Little Movie Glossary*, Rogert Ebert, comp. (Andrews & McMeel, 1994).

14. Most movies are segmented into "shots" that fit together thematically or visually. This series of connected shots is called a *sequence*. It corresponds roughly to a scene in a play. Opening sequences in films frequently establish the tone and style for the entire movie. Often an important story segment is presented even before we see the film credits. Our interest is piqued, and we wonder if we can guess where the movie is going.

15. The award-winning movie *Fargo* (1996) begins in a similar manner. We're caught in a white-out storm that erases time and place. This is fitting preparation for a movie with complex storytelling and themes.

16. The function of a *voice-over* in a movie is to provide helpful background and sometimes offer spectators interpretations for events. Martin Scorsese *(Taxi Driver, The Age of Innocence)* learned it from Robert Bresson, whose *Diary of a Country Priest* we will examine in chapter 4. In *GoodFellas*, for instance, the narrator provides a moral perspective and a distance from the events on screen, which represent intense violence and treachery.

17. Each of the women will blossom by the end of the film. But none of them will emerge as a conventional movie heroine like Sigourney Weaver's powerful Ripley in the *Alien* movies. Hollywood studios (and many independent studios) bank on their stars, which means that films must have heroes or heroines to capture audience attention. This is a time-honored storytelling practice; we love stories about King Arthur and the Knights of the Round Table and other tales of romance and heroism. The *Alien* movies have established women as viable action heroes. These particular films also have a strong flavor of savior, redeemer, mother, and other religious themes, as do other space movies such as *Star Wars, Star Trek, Dune,* and *Stargate*. (*See* chapter 3.)

18. The use of photographs is more effective than the usual film flashback, which may or may not present us with the "truth." In *Dead Man Walking*, for instance, we see a number of flashbacks of the murder scene, but each of them presents a false version of the truth. Thrillers and mysteries make use of flashbacks to fill in missing plot information. The lying or misleading flashback can add layers of complication to our viewing experience, as in *Usual Suspects*: Why are we so eager to believe what we see and hear? A creative use of flashbacks to present characters' versions of an event is found in *Rashomon* (1950), by the Japanese director Akira Kurosawa.

19. *Eyeline match:* a character looks out of the frame one way, and in the next frame another character looks back at exactly that level. *Match on action:* two separate framings of the same action are cut together "at the same moment in the gesture," making the gesture seem "uninterrupted" (*Film Art*, 495).

20. The biggest changes in the film come for the women who grew up

depending on men for survival and happiness. This dependence made them passive and fearful. Faced with death, they reclaim a sense of adventure. (This same point is made in *Thelma and Louise,* but in *Strangers,* without the violence.)

21. Thanks to Anthony Tang for his analysis of the role of the bird songs in Constance's rejuvenation, Spring 1997.

22. Patricia Mellencamp compares women's lives to those of the nomads, who as "displaced persons" must create home through myths and story (*A Fine Romance: Five Ages of Film Feminism* [Philadelphia: Temple Univ. Press, 1995], 252-3).

2. Authenticity

1. *The Confessions of St. Augustine,* trans. Rex Warner, Book VII, ch. 10 (New York: Penguin, 1963).

2. *The Institutes,* ed. John T. McNeill (Philadelphia: Westminster Press, 1960), 35-6.

3. Ibid., 38.

4. For theorist Roland Barthes, "story meant secrets, usually sexual secrets linked to identity." This is a summary from his work *S/Z,* referenced (and criticized) in Patricia Mellencamp, *A Fine Romance,* 133: "The secret triggered the pursuit of the truth, which was delayed, hidden." Your grandmother's frustrating anecdotes, filled with digressions, illustrate one aspect of this insight into storytelling: the delaying technique that makes the punchline the sweeter (and, in a film, spins the tale out over at least ninety minutes).

5. Tampering with memories is an idea dear to science fiction. *Total Recall* is built on it, and *Blade Runner* considers it as the ultimate insult of "creating" human life through science. *Men in Black* spoofs the whole idea by furnishing the heroes with a little flashlight that erases memories of experience and understanding.

6. I am reminded here of medieval and Renaissance art. Agnes lies cold and hard on her bed like the knights and ladies whose carved stone images lie in so many European churches; the pastor is like one of the praying figures who surround such a figure in religious triptychs.

7. From the film's subtitles.

8. *Four Stories by Ingmar Bergman,* trans. Alan Blair (New York: Doubleday, 1976), 75.

9. I am grateful to David Pomeroy for this insight in his unpublished manuscript, "The Vision of Ingmar Bergman," 271.

10. Quoted in Charles B. Ketcham, *The Influence of Existentialism on Ingmar Bergman: An Analysis of the Theological Ideas Shaping a Filmmaker's Art.*

Studies in Art and Religious Interpretation, Vol. 5. (Lewiston/Queenston: The Edwin Mellen Press, date unknown), 308.

11. Ibid. Pomeroy is much less confident that the film presents a vision of wholeness. He writes: "In his more optimistic moments Bergman finds that wholeness is already there just waiting to be discovered: 'Every human being has a sort of dignity of wholeness in him and out of that develops relationships to other human beings, tensions, misunderstandings, tenderness, coming in contact, touching and being touched, the cutting off of contact . . .' (Pomeroy, 179)."

Usually Bergman's films show a lack of wholeness, Pomeroy comments. People try to complete themselves through others, but this is doomed to fail.

12. As Freeman Patterson has said, "Photographers reveal something of themselves in every photo they take." Overheard on "Morningsong" interview with Patterson, Canada, August 4, 1997.

13. An example of crosscutting that is used to build suspense is the pursuit through the woods of Clint Eastwood's cat burglar in *Absolute Power*: first Eastwood, sliding down a rope; then his pursuers; then Eastwood, heading off into the woods; then the pursuers using infrared glasses to spot him in the dark; and so forth. Crosscutting may also be used to follow simultaneous story lines, or, as here, to allow us access to each woman's response as Hortense reveals her existence.

14. *Dead time* is what most moviemakers avoid: long seconds with no conversation. *Terminator 2* and *The Rock* have no dead time. *Secrets & Lies* lets characters pause, take a breath, be embarrassed, scramble for what to say next—just as in life.

15. In movies, stairs often indicate moments of passage or of impending discovery. Cf. *Blade Runner's* elaborate staircase, or the stairways in movies as dissimilar as Orson Welles's *The Magnificent Ambersons,* Hitchcock's *Vertigo,* and *My Left Foot.*

16. The medium shot is the most common distance shot. It allows the viewer to figure out the relationship between characters (which often involves a power struggle). It also provides a fairly good picture of the setting while keeping the viewer close enough to stay interested in the characters.

3. Alienation

1. Michael Kilian, "Bleak Summer," in *Chicago Tribune* (July 24, 1997), section 5, 8C. Kilian quotes from Patrick McGilligan's *Fritz Lang: The Nature of the Beast* in his entertaining article. *Nihilism* (the rejection of commonly held moral ideals) is often applied loosely to films such as *Kids* (1996), which present a dismal picture of society and appear to offer little hope for change. For scholar of Black history Cornel West,

recovery from nihilism resembles recovery from addiction; both are "diseases of the soul." Quoted in Patricia Mellencamp, *A Fine Romance,* 247.

2. The surgery shown in *Face/Off* presents yet another ethical problem. Recently, an FBI informant instrumental in solving a drug case was subjected to face-changing surgery as part of his new identity. He died during surgery (*News Hour with Jim Lehrer,* September 3, 1997).

3. Kilian, "Bleak Summer."

4. As one spectator commented to me after this movie, it's difficult these days for directors to find villains that don't have a powerful lobby in Washington. Americans seem particularly eager to fit characters into types: serial killer, sociopath, corporate lawyer, evil or good cop. Recently the issue has resurfaced with the embassy bombings in Kenya and Tanzania and with the release of *The Siege,* in which Arab-Americans are forced into detention camps for fear of terrorist attacks in New York City. See *New York Times* (November 1, 1998, AR 17), 12, 20.

5. See Oliver O'Donovan, *Desire of the Nations: Rediscovering the Roots of Political Theology,* (Cambridge: Cambridge Univ. Press, 1996), esp. 74.

6. In the Hebrew Scriptures, Yahweh is the advocate for or defender of the sufferer against the chaos of the universe. When this confidence in an advocate (or in Christ, the mediator) disappears, then perhaps narratives substitute an avenger-hero. See the discussion of *Unforgiven,* chapter 5.

7. The movie *Breakdown* violates this basic sense of fair play by killing a defenseless man. He may be the villain, but part of the code of justice includes generosity to the enemy, giving him his day in court.

8. The troubles on Mir were "the summer's only genuine galactic soap opera," one article proclaimed (*New York Times,* August 17, 1997), A-1.

9. Quoted in *New York Times,* July 6, 1997.

10. Andrew Gordon, "Star Wars: A Myth for Our Time," in *Screening the Sacred: Religion, Myth, and Ideology in Popular American Film,* ed. Joel W. Martin and Conrad E. Ostwalt, Jr. (Boulder: Westview Press, 1995), 82.

11. The series creator, Gene Roddenberry, was quite specific about his intentions. *Star Trek* differs from another popular and well-constructed TV phenomenon, *The X-Files,* in its consistent affirmation of human values such as love, loyalty, reflection, intelligence, and courage. In *The X-Files,* there is a feeling that humans are under constant threat from dark, powerful forces of evil that are all around them. Even the hero and heroine in *X-Files* have not escaped infection. And even more than in classic film noir movies such as *The Big Sleep,* we wonder what keeps the heroes going.

12. Neither the films nor the television episodes downplay the intricacies of scientific knowledge or dumb down the characters' intelligence. The series has had four incarnations. The original ran from 1966–1969 and featured Captain Kirk and Spock. *Star Trek: The Next Generation* featured Captain Jean-Luc Picard and Data. *Star Trek: Deep Space Nine* and *Star Trek: Voyager* are still running, *Voyager* being noteworthy and groundbreaking for having a female captain.

13. Curiously, neither *Solaris* nor *Stalker* appears on the Vatican's list of the forty-five greatest movies of all time, but *2001: A Space Odyssey* does (for artistic merit). Tarkovsky chose the space theme for *Solaris* in part because he rebelled against the sterility of *2001*, which seemed to him to glorify human technological achievements. The scene I remember most vividly from *2001* is the one where the hero disconnects the master computer. Somehow the computer (which winds down its life singing "Daisy, Daisy") seems more human than the ice-cold astronaut.

14. In *Crime and Punishment*, the villain Svidrigailov (whose story and suicide lead the hero Raskolnikov to admit his guilt to himself and turn himself in to the authorities) tells that he had seduced a young, innocent girl, then had revealed to her that what they had done together was vile and sinful. She had killed herself in self-loathing.

15. In *Superman II*, devastated by the death of his beloved Lois Lane, Superman actually turns the globe backward, reversing time to allow him to undo the past. *Groundhog Day* plays this theme in a lighter key, as does *Back to the Future.*

16. See Johnson and Petrie, *Andrei Tarkovsky: A Visual Fugue*, 102-3.

17. From *Sculpting in Time: Reflections on the Cinema*, trans. Kitty Hunter Blair (New York: Knopf, 1987), 165-8. The artist's commitment to a higher goal, that of presenting "truth" rather than the trivial, is what makes art (including great movies) potentially "religious." The most lovely of Tarkovsky's movies, *Andrei Roublev*, examines the artist's commitment to his work in the world as a divine calling.

18. Thanks to Meagan Rawlins for pointing out that Deckard's name may refer to the French philosopher René Descartes: "I think, therefore I am."

19. *New York Times*, July 6, 1997, H-18.

20. Thanks to the insights of Professor Robert Jewett.

4. Vocation

1. Lecture at Northwestern University, May 17, 1997.

2. See P. Adams Sitney, *Modernist Montage* (New York: Columbia Univ. Press, 1990). Thanks to Tom Gunning for the reference.

3. Like us, the movie spectators, the priest seems to identify with first one person in his life, then another. He is like Dr. Delbende and the young Chantal, who despair; Seraphita, child of poverty; the Countess, who fights God. For a fascinating recasting of *Diary*, see Martin Scorsese's *Taxi Driver* (1976).

4. Thanks to the students of Ken Vaux's Spring 1997 ethics class for thoughts on *Wall Street*.

5. Manichaeanism was an early religion that formed around the ideas of the Persian Mani.

6. Robert Coles has used the similar film *A Bronx Tale* (De Niro, 1993) in working on values clarification with adolescents. In *Tale*, a boy has two fathers, an "ethically demanding biological one" and a man who operates "outside the law." Coles comments: "We link arms in our hearts, our guts, with this youth, who is torn by various attachments, loyalties, desires, and yearnings, and who lives in a world where good and evil can't be utterly, neatly, conveniently distinguished . . ." (18). A moving story of a fifteen-year-old boy in Belgium alters this plot slightly. In *La Promesse* (*The Promise*, 1996), the hero must choose between his father, who loves him but is a crook, and the safety of an illegal immigrant from Nigeria and her little baby. The movie poses *vocation* as a central issue but almost immediately changes the definition of the word from "mechanic" or "smuggler of human labor" to "personhood"—what kind of person he will become morally.

7. *New York Times* (May 18, 1997), business section. The article continues: "These attributes failed him in negotiations with his own daughters," who have been attempting to seize their shares of his empire. Negotiations seems a sad word, at odds within family or household.

8. Thomas Cahill, *How the Irish Saved Civilization: The Untold Story of Ireland's Heroic Role from the Fall of Rome to the Rise of Medieval Europe* (New York: Doubleday, 1995), 47.

9. The quotation is from J. H. Newman, used in the *Shorter Oxford English Dictionary*, 3rd ed., 2332.

10. Rosemary Radford Ruether, *Gaia and God* (HarperSanFrancisco, 1992), 198-9.

5. Integrity

1. *John Wayne's America: The Politics of Celebrity* (New York: Simon and Schuster, 1997).

2. *Manifest Destiny* is defined as a "catchword implying divine sanction for the territorial expansion of the young nation," *Encyclopedia Americana*, vol. 18 (Danbury, Conn.: Grolier Inc., 1993), 235. First published 1829.

3. Wills, 302.

4. Ibid., 302.

5. From the TNT special *Big Guns Talk: The Story of the Western,* July 27, 1997.

6. *Old West and Reality: A Showdown,* in *New York Times* (July 23, 1997). Joseph Conrad faced this human failing in his famous short novel *The Heart of Darkness.*

7. *Oxford English Dictionary,* vol. V (Oxford: Clarendon Press, first published 1933, reprinted 1961), 368.

8. Whether Westerns have helped to sustain an antigovernment mentality is a matter that Robert Jewett takes up in his work.

9. As the descendant of Civil War soldiers, let me offer some perspective on Ethan's actions. Few soldiers on either side survived to return to their homes. Most came from desperately poor households, from tiny farming communities hit hard by war privations; wealthy men bought substitutes to serve for them or received "exemptions" from service. Francis Anderson and Andrew Edinger, two examples, had fourteen children each to support at home and enlisted in part to support their families.

10. Pauline Kael compared Eastwood's *Pale Rider* with *Shane* (1951). See "Old Movies," *NYT* (October 19, 1997). The quote about Eastwood's persona (the character carefully nursed by Eastwood's mentors Don Siegel and Sergio Leone) is from a conversation with Tom Gunning.

11. The Kid suggests the infamous Billy the Kid, a self-created screwball who murdered randomly until his death in 1881 at age twenty-one. He was one of our first media stars, catching the public's imagination. His (embellished) image is perpetuated through endless movies such as *The Left-Handed Gun,* with Paul Newman. There's an intriguing interplay between the Kid's age in this film in 1880 (about twenty) and the name William Munny. Billy the Kid's real name was William Bonney. Is this another "What-If" situation: What if Billy the Kid had been sickened by killing after his first murder, as The Schofield Kid is in this film?

12. *Unforgiven* is rich with religious imagery. This sequence is one example: Ned holding Will's head resembles paintings of the Virgin Mary cradling the head of the dead Christ. Will lies at the point of death three days, sustained by Ned's tender care and by the food and water of the prostitutes. I needn't add that the shack where he lies dying is situated "outside the camp"—far removed from the so-called civilization of Big Whiskey.

13. *Embodying Forgiveness* (Grand Rapids, Mich.: Eerdmans, 1995), 73.

14. Interview on Internet (plaza.net/zone/mrcranky/interviews/sayles.html).

15. In *Mr. Deeds Goes to Town* (1936), Gary Cooper plays a wide-eyed, straight-talking guy who inherits a fortune and manages to preserve his integrity.

6. Purity of Heart

1. The Feast of Fools flourished in France in various forms until the sixteenth century but was stamped out in England at the end of the fourteenth century. The time of the highjinks seems to have been Christmas or New Year's. See Sandra Billington, *The Social History of the Fool* (New York: St. Martin's Press, 1984), 1-5. Court fools were hired by early kings such as Henry VIII to remind them of their own mortality; Russian nobility in the nineteenth and early twentieth centuries were fascinated by the "holy fools" that roamed Russia, whose simplicity and poverty were seen in part as bringing them in touch with God.

2. Professor Pierre Prigent of Strasbourg, France, discussed this idea in a lecture on Tarkovsky's last film, *Sacrifice*. In this movie, the hero sacrifices all his worldly goods—and his sanity—to save the world.

3. *Praise of Folly*, trans. Betty Radice (Penguin, 1991), 125-6.

4. Soren Kierkegaard, *Purity of Heart Is to Will One Thing*, trans. Douglas V. Steere (New York: Harper & Bros. Harper Torchlight ed., 1956), 175.

5. Matthew Giunti, "Forrest Gump: Ignorance Is Bliss," *Christian Century* (May 15, 1996), 548.

6. *The Moral Intelligence of Children* (New York: Random House, 1997).

7. *Federico Fellini: Variety Lights to La Dolce Vita* (Boston: Twayne Publisher, 1984), 61.

8. Ibid. 41.

9. Mark Caro, *Chicago Tribune* (April 18, 1997), Tempo section, 1.

10. Thanks to Dan Burns and others for this observation. The anguished hero of *A Perfect World* (Eastwood, 1993) struggles in a similar way with his memory of his father's violent abuse.

11. Ray Pride, film reviewer for *New City* (June 26, 1997), Section 2, page 32.

12. Thanks to the insights of my Garrett class on "Teaching Film in the Congregation," Fall 1997.

7. Celebration

1. Frank C. Senn, *Christian Liturgy: Catholic and Evangelical* (Minneapolis: Fortress Press, 1997), 7.

2. See *The Historical Jesus: The Life of a Mediterranean Jewish Peasant* (New York: HarperCollins, paperback, 1992), 341. Crossan quotes here from Edward Klosinski.

3. Thanks to sermons by Don Chatfield, Dwight Vogel, and Robert Jewett for variations on this rich idea.

4. From a sermon delivered in Garrett-Evangelical Theological Seminary chapel, February 28, 1995. See also Wayne Meek.

5. Perversion of communion's essential generosity—turning the feast into a tool of discrimination and punishment—is presented in *Breaking the Waves*. The pastor of the heroine, Bess, intones that if there is one commandment you do not obey, you have no place at the Lord's Table. As that disturbing movie insists, however, to be cut off from communion, cut off from grace, is to be cut off from life. The film strongly affirms that redemption can come nonetheless to the least likely persons—in this case, to a simple young woman, who has become a prostitute in the belief that her "sins" will save the life of the man she loves.

6. *Gullah* and *Geechee* are both tribal names from West Africa. "Gullah" refers specifically to the dialect, a Sea Island creole derived from the Ibo language among other West African languages, created in part as a trading language. Parts of the dialogue in the movie are in Gullah, or a mixture of Gullah and standard English. Because of its isolated location, this island preserved many customs and speech patterns from the heritage of its people as well as from the early English settlers. (See *Encyclopaedia Britannica* and Dash's screenplay, *Daughters of the Dust: The Making of An African American Woman's Film* [New Press, 1992].)

7. For a fascinating variation on this mode of storytelling, I highly recommend Clint Eastwood's brilliant film *Bird*, about jazz legend Charlie Parker. Eastwood sets stories within stories and frames within frames—much as a grandmother or grandfather might add color to a central tale by embellishing it with odd bits of character or local color, or might take it farther back in time: "But that was before the opera house in St. Petersburg burned down in 1871," as my old friend John Kline used to say.

8. From the video soundtrack and from the screenplay, 82-83.

9. Again, see Eastwood's *Bird*, where Charlie Parker pawns his precious saxophone to rent a white horse to carry away his sweetheart.

10. Patricia Mellencamp, *A Fine Romance: Four Ages of Film Feminism* (Philadelphia: Temple University Press, 1995), 244.

11. The phrase is adapted from "The Sin of Servanthood and the Deliverance of Discipleship," in Emilie M. Townes, ed. *A Troubling in My Soul: Womanist Perspectives on Evil and Suffering* (Maryknoll, N.Y. [Orbis], 1993). Thanks to Heather Grennan for pointing out this idea.

12. Mellencamp, 240.

13. Ray Pride, *New City* (July 31, 1997), 2/38.

14. From the Internet, supplemented by my own memory of the dialogue.

8. Healing: A Film Diary

1. Janet Maslin, *New York Times* (December 30, 1996), Section B.

2. Michael Ondaatje, *The English Patient* (New York: Random House, 1992; Vintage edition 1993).

3. My thanks to Dorothee Soelle for this insight. In a sermon given at Garrett-Evangelical Theological Seminary May 15, 1997, she spoke of "turning our wishes" and praying to be cleansed "from the will to power."

4. *New International Dictionary of New Testament Theology,* Vol. 2 (Grand Rapids, Mich.: Zondervan Pub. House, 1986 ed.), 167.

5. Ondaatje, 89. The film shows us the patient's edgy, self-referential, chatty style, whereas the novel sometimes quotes his words, sometimes tells us what he said. "Showing" versus "telling" in storytelling is discussed in Wayne Booth's classic study *The Rhetoric of Fiction* (Chicago and New York: Univ. of Chicago Press, 1971 and 1983).

6. David Aaron Murray, "The English Patient Plays Casablanca," *First Things* (May 1997); 10.

7. John Ford wrestled with this problem in *The Searchers,* and Clint Eastwood exposed its multiple sides in *Unforgiven.*

8. That is, he is given a dose of morphine to kill his pain, first effect, but his central nervous system will be depressed and he will die, second effect. This is discussed in Vaux & Vaux, *Dying Well in the Late Twentieth Century.* Another film representation of the situation is *Un coeur en hiver (A Heart in Winter).*

9. That is, the law only has binding force within your camp; it is an artificial structure without inherent validity.

10. Thanks to Bert Vaux for these suggestions.

11. One of the most powerful examinations of such a morality shift is Joseph Conrad's novel *Heart of Darkness.*

12. Christina Maranci has suggested that this bright red wrapper might be from Demels, a Viennese bakery famous for its *Suchertort* (sweet cake).

13. Metaphor works by triggering such associations. Movies can highlight the ways in which one image (a rumpled sheet; a plum) multiplies into many (hospital beds; war wounded; desert sand. Or with the plum: feast; sweetness; mother's care; springtime garden; new life).

14. Thanks to Caroline Portaro for insights into Almásy's heroism.

15. A footnote to the use of linguist-as-detective device in *Indiana Jones* and *Stargate* is that in the two world wars, the best source for code-breakers was university departments of classics and other languages—notably from Oxford and Cambridge. Linguists now are in demand in computer technology and artificial intelligence. Thanks to Dong Fu for the computer tip.

16. Again I refer to the fine book by Margaret Miles and to Martha Nussbaum's work on Greek drama.

17. *Purity of Heart,* 161.

18. In some ways, Kip is set up in the film to parallel the Count. Both are risk-takers; both have tunnel vision; both are men of quest. But where

the limited vision of the Count leads to the deaths of people he loves, Kip's concentration is limited only when he focuses intently on the secrets of the death-machines.

19. David Aaron Murray, 10-11.
20. *Purity of Heart*, 161.
21. *The Patient's Ordeal* (Bloomington: Indiana Univ. Press, 1991), 23. Dax quoted on p. 22.
22. This is in the novel. In the film, Kip's uneasiness with India's colonial status is expressed when he is reading Kipling's *Kim* to the English patient.
23. See Edward W. Said, *Culture and Imperialism* (New York: Vintage Books, 1994), for a discussion of the issues of colonialism and nineteenth century literature. See especially the section on Jane Austen, 80-97.

BASIC FILM TERMS*

crane: a shot from above, providing us a bird's-eye view of the action

crosscutting: shots that cut from one action to another. These may emphasize parallel events (and thus provide contrast), or they may build suspense, as with a chase scene

diegesis: the total story world—the context, history, and background events that relate to the film events (World War II, the frontier, outer space, etc.)

frame: a single image on a strip of film

framing: this may refer to the way the shot is composed or may refer to the movie's "bookends" (a shot or sequence at the end of the film that echoes the shot or sequence at the beginning)

mise-en-scène: all that you see before you on the screen—everything that was put there before the camera began to roll

narrative: the telling of the story

narrative style: the way the film unfolds

narrator: who tells the story (there may not be anyone)

pan: the camera is on a stationary tripod, scanning the space

plot: all events "directly presented to us" in the film. In this book, "plot" refers to a basic summary of the movie's occurrences and characters, not necessarily in the order in which they appear in the film.

sequence: a series of shots. This roughly corresponds to a scene in a play—a group of shots that are related by theme or action

shot or **take:** the camera rolls on, with the shot unbroken by editing

shot/counter shot: we see first a shot of the person speaking, then we see who is being spoken to

story (fabula): what we construct in our minds about the background of characters and events from what we see and hear (sometimes called the *diegesis*, the "recounted story")

style: all the components of the film—lighting, camera distance, acting style, editing pace, costumes, color, etc.

three-point lighting: light is carefully manipulated to give an effect appropriate to the narrative—key lighting, backlighting, and fill light for softness create different atmospheres. Some directors such as Clint Eastwood prefer to use natural light

tracking shot: the camera moves around, changing the "frame" within which we see persons or objects

voice-over: commentary on the plot that is provided by someone outside the frame

* For further detail, see David Bordwell and Kristin Thompson, *Film Art: An Introduction*, 5th ed. (New York: McGraw Hill, 1997), 477-82.